S·T·A·R·T
T·H·E·M
THINKING

A Handbook of Classroom Strategies for the Early Years

Robin Fogarty & Kay Opeka

SkyLight

TRAINING AND PUBLISHING,
Arlington Heights, Illinois

Start Them Thinking:
A Handbook of Classroom Strategies for the Early Years
Second Edition

IRI/Skylight Training and Publishing, Inc.
2626 S. Clearbrook Dr.
Arlington Heights, IL 60005
800-348-4474 or 847-290-6600
Fax 847-290-6609
info@iriskylight.com
http://www.iriskylight.com

© 1988 IRI/Skylight Training and Publishing, Inc.

Production coordination and computer graphics: Brian Larson
Type composition: Donna Ramirez
Graphics: Jim Arthur and Mike Melasi
Book design: Bruce Leckie

ISBN 0-932935-52-4

0561C-3-98CHG
Item number 613
06 05 04 03 02 01 00 99 98   15 14 13 12 11 10 9 8 7 6 5 4 3

Acknowledgments

We would like to express appreciation to several special educators whose direct or indirect influence helped shape this book:

Dr. Arthur Costa of the University of California at Sacramento, who promotes the concept of setting a thinking environment in the classroom.

Dr. Barry Beyer of George Mason University in Virginia, who advocates the teaching of explicit thinking skills.

Drs. Roger and David Johnson, University of Minnesota, who mentor our thinking about cooperative learning and structured interactions.

Dr. Ronald Brandt, Executive Editor, ASCD, who continues to address the need to teach for, of, and about thinking.

James Bellanca, Executive Director of The IRI Group, whose interest and support make the final realization of this project possible.

Our sincere thanks to these individuals for their leadership and impact in teaching for cooperative and cognitive behaviors.

Contents

START THEM THINKING CREATIVELY

START THEM PROBLEM SOLVING AND DECISION MAKING

Preface

It is our belief that the ability to think critically and creatively need not be reserved for older students. In fact, very young children occupy much of their time exploring the world by asking questions, seeking patterns, hypothesizing, inferring, generalizing, and ingeniously solving problems through their own versions of logical reasoning.

Think for a moment about the skill observations of the two year old who sees a "fly" and says "bird" because he sees a pattern of behavior similar in both. Or think of kindergarten children who are bombarded with a classroom environment and curriculum that requires analysis of similarities and differences, sequencing objects, finding color patterns, and hypothesizing what might happen next in a story.

The same pattern follows into the other primary grades. Visualize the skilled problem-solvers on the playground who defy gravity and find clever ways to climb every high object in sight. Or, consider the understanding of young minds that is so insightful, that it's disturbing. One third grade child remarks that he has never been asked to read the "long parts" because he can't read fast. Another fourth grader sighs in frustration because she never has time to read in school because she is too busy working on "busy work."

To present thought-provoking lessons, as well as explicit thinking skills to young people who are so ready to learn, is

more than desirable, it is imperative. Young minds relish
analysis and creativity. By introducing youngsters to the rigor
and fun of skillful thinking early in their academic careers,
we are giving them tools for life-long learning.

To that purpose—to *Start Them Thinking* in the early years, we
present the motivational activities in this book.

Ready? Set? Go!

                                        Kay & Robin

Introduction

Before you dive into the activities presented here to *Start Them Thinking*, we want to suggest a rationale for the thinking focus, and provide a brief overview of the key elements of the thinking classroom. In addition, we will provide an outline of the lesson format and suggest how to use this book to start very young children thinking.

Twenty years ago, Alvin Toffler startled the literary community with his best seller, *Future Shock*. In that document he boldly predicted the skills needed by the students of the future. He stated that students need the following skills:

- Learning to learn

- Learning to relate

- Learning to choose

Today, we see the educational community focusing on these very skills. Metacognitive processing helps students learn about their learning and think about their thinking. Cooperative learning models stress social skills and collegial behaviors as students engage in team efforts. Finally, information-processing models that stress problem solving and decision making are pervading the curricula from pre-school to college.

What does this mean to us? Well, simply put, thinking teachers have thinking classrooms. To engage children in higher-order cognitive processing, cooperative social behaviors, and a predisposition to lifelong learning, the teacher must consider four key questions:

1. How do I set the climate for a thinking classroom?

2. What are the thinking skills embedded in my curriculum and how do I teach the explicit skills of thinking?

3. How will I structure student interaction with other students and with the materials to foster thinking?

4. How will I lead children to think about their thinking metacognitively?

Let's look at these four areas more closely.

THE THINKING CLASSROOM

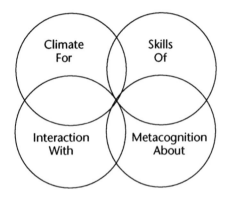

Setting the CLIMATE for Thinking:

❏ Is the room arranged to foster student interaction?

❏ Am I visible, available, and mobile?

❏ Am I asking "how" and "why" questions that require in-depth student responses?

❏ Do I use the wait-time, 3-second pause after asking questions and following student responses to allow time for thinking?

Teaching EXPLICIT SKILLS of Thinking:

❏ Am I identifying the thinking skills inherent in my curriculum?

❏ Am I taking advantage of the "teachable moments" by developing these thinking skills explicitly?

❏ Am I asking students to generate ideas with creative thinking skills: brainstorming, predicting, visualizing, and associating?

❑ Am I asking students to evaluate ideas with critical thinking skills: classifying, comparing and contrasting, and sequencing?

STRUCTURED INTERACTION with Cooperative Thinking:

❑ Am I utilizing think/pair/share strategies?

❑ Am I structuring interdependent cooperative groups and focusing on social behaviors?

❑ Am I using a repertoire of individualistic, competitive, and cooperative models of interaction?

❑ Am I using graphic organizers and mnemonic devices to help students interact with the material? (Venn diagrams, webs, matrices)

Processing Thinking METACOGNITIVELY:

❑ Are students required to plan, monitor, and evaluate their own behavior?

❑ Am I asking questions that lead students into reflective thinking:

  • What did you do well?

  • What would you do differently?

❑ Am I using art logs or work folders to document changes in student thinking over time?

❑ Am I making student thinking patterns visible through discussion strategies and instructional techniques?

HOW TO USE THIS BOOK

With this broad framework in mind, the lessons in *Start Them Thinking* have been divided into four major areas:

1. Start Them Thinking

2. Start Them Thinking Critically

3. Start Them Thinking Creatively

4. Start Them Problem Solving and Decision Making

Lessons in the first section, **Start Them Thinking**, focus on readiness activities that lay the groundwork for future lessons. Active listening strategies, cooperative skills, and questioning techniques provide the curriculum emphasis for these early lessons.

Start Them Thinking Critically provides 15 lessons that start analytical and evaluative mental processing by the youngsters. The lessons in this section are concerned with organizing and analyzing data, comparing, contrasting, classifying, sequencing, and prioritizing.

Just as students are led to think critically in the second set of lessons, **Start Them Thinking Creatively** leads students into generative and productive mental processes. This third section develops lessons that ask students to behave creatively by brainstorming, visualizing, personifying, inferring, and using analogies.

Finally, in the last section of the book, **Start Them Problem Solving and Decision Making**, lessons focus on the integration of both critical, analytical skills and creative, generative skills into the more complex processes of problem solving and decision making.

HOW THE LESSONS ARE ORGANIZED

Each lesson is outlined in the same manner.

BACKGROUND: A brief rationale and theory base is included for each skill activity.

THINKING SKILL: The specific micro-skill is named.

FOCUS ACTIVITY: A short, anticipatory activity is suggested to set the stage for the skill introduction.

OBJECTIVE: The cognitive/cooperative skill of the lesson is explicitly stated.

INPUT: Directions, instructions, and materials needed for the lesson are discussed.

ACTIVITY: The thinking activity of lesson content is developed.

METACOGNITIVE DISCUSSION: Reflective questions and discussion ideas are listed.

CLOSURE: A follow-up, independent task provides closure to the lesson.

Use the lessons as they appear or create your own. As you work with the materials in *Start Them Thinking*, you may want to SCAMPER the lessons for further extension. Ask yourself, how might I:

Substitute another topic or concept.
Combine with another activity.
Adapt for another content.
Modify for younger or older.
Put to another use.
Eliminate or elaborate a part of the lesson.
Rearrange or reverse part of the lesson.

Also, to provide a guide to the questioning levels, included here is a comment on three-story intellects from Oliver Wendell Holmes and some questioning prompts for quick reference.

There are one-story intellects, two-story intellects,
and three-story intellects with skylights.
All fact collectors who have no aim beyond their facts are one-story men.
Two-story men compare, reason, generalize,
using the labor of fact collectors as their own.
Three-story men idealize, imagine, predict—
their best illumination comes from above the skylight.

The Three-Story Intellect

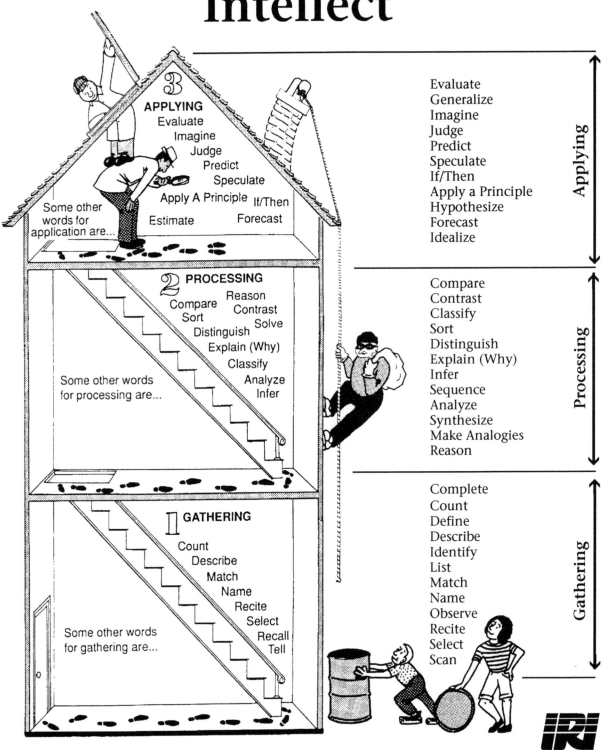

3 APPLYING
Evaluate
Imagine
Judge
Predict
Speculate
Apply A Principle   If/Then
Estimate   Forecast

Some other words for application are...

2 PROCESSING
Reason
Compare   Contrast
Sort
Solve
Distinguish
Explain (Why)
Classify
Analyze
Infer

Some other words for processing are...

1 GATHERING
Count
Describe
Match
Name
Recite
Select
Recall
Tell

Some other words for gathering are...

Applying
Evaluate
Generalize
Imagine
Judge
Predict
Speculate
If/Then
Apply a Principle
Hypothesize
Forecast
Idealize

Processing
Compare
Contrast
Classify
Sort
Distinguish
Explain (Why)
Infer
Sequence
Analyze
Synthesize
Make Analogies
Reason

Gathering
Complete
Count
Define
Describe
Identify
List
Match
Name
Observe
Recite
Select
Scan

Start ThemThinking

Two Plus Two Equals More (2-4-6-8)

BACKGROUND

To promote thinking in the classroom, student-to-student interactions in paired partners is an effective strategy. But to guide quality time during partner sharings, young students need to practice listening skills as well as articulation skills. An easy way to facilitate active listening behaviors is to give students a *reason to listen*. This activity requires careful listening because the listening partner has to retell his partner's story.

THINKING SKILL

Active Listening

FOCUS ACTIVITY

Ask students to identify a partner and find a spot where they can sit "eye-to-eye" and "knee-to-knee." Identify the speaker and the listener (e.g., the shortest partner speaks first, etc.). Ask the speaker to describe his or her bedroom. Then, instruct the listener to do everything he can think of NOT to listen. After a minute or two, reverse the roles.

Once the giggles have subsided, ask the students: 1) How did it feel when your partner didn't listen? 2) What are things that told you she or he wasn't listening?

From the negative behaviors, your students are now ready to list the positive behaviors of a good listener.

OBJECTIVE	To identify helpful listening behaviors.

INPUT	Make a list on chart paper, eliciting from students "what it looks like" when someone is listening. The list might include:

1. looking at the person
2. nodding
3. not interrupting
4. leaning toward the speaker
5. smiling
6. asking questions (to clarify)
7. not doing other things

ACTIVITY	Instructions: (This may be done on a second day depending on age and attention of students)

1. "Find your partner again. This time you will share a Show and Tell (Bring and Brag) item with your partner."

2. "It's going to be important for you to listen closely because you will have to retell your partner's information."

3. Let each of the two partners share their Show and Tell item.

4. Instruct them to find another set of partners. Now, the twosomes become foursomes.

5. In the foursomes, each person tells about his or her partner's Show and Tell item. In this way, the Show and Tell articulation experience becomes also a focused listening experience, setting the groundwork for a thinking classroom of quality interactions.

Extension: The foursomes can become "eights" if your groups can handle further extensions.

METACOGNITIVE DISCUSSION	Ask students to share with a partner some times, both in and out of schools, when they need to listen.

CLOSURE

In a wrap-around the room, invite students to tell why listening is sometimes a hard thing to do.

Watch Us Work!

BACKGROUND	Cooperative groups increase interaction, involvement, and output. Millions of dollars are spent on corporate think tanks, government task forces, and research teams for education. Research in *Circles of Learning* by David and Roger Johnson suggests classroom models in which groups of 3-4 children are assigned roles and responsibilities. Young children can work in groups with these responsibilities. The classroom teacher may introduce roles as the children are developmentally capable of accepting and performing these roles. The task only needs to be adapted to applicable skills, interests, and abilities...kindergarten children can handle materials manager and observer (reporter) roles without problems.

THINKING SKILL	Group Interaction

FOCUS ACTIVITY	Ask students to get into groups of four (4) by finding three other people who are wearing the same color.

OBJECTIVE	Children will work in groups of 3-4 to focus on role responsibility and the process of interaction.

INPUT

The four roles integrated into the thinking lessons are:

LEADER: Keep group on task.

MATERIALS MANAGER: Assemble, replenish, and return needed materials.

RECORDER: Writes, tallies, and charts information generated by the group.

OBSERVER/TIMEKEEPER: Observes processes and reports for the group.

IMPORTANT: Be sure observer knows what is to be reported— the product or the process.

Selecting roles can become inventive. For example, you could select the child who has the most letters in her last name, has the most buttons on his clothes, or has the closest birthday— then name the role _____.

When children are responsible for assigned roles, the teacher has time to observe behaviors, provide task assistance, and intervene when absolutely necessary.

ACTIVITY

1. Each group has a different set of building "things" (Legos, Tinker Toys, Lincoln Logs, Snap-ums, large primary blocks, whatever). Build a school in an alotted time period (for non-readers, non-writers).

2. Each group chooses a favorite fairytale or story and does a mapping (see: "Start With Me," a strategy in this book).

3. Each group has one large piece of chart paper with a word such as "Valentines," "Stegosaurus," or "Marshmallow" printed at the top. Using only the letters in the assigned word, have children write down as many other words as they can spell from the letters in the larger word as time permits.

METACOGNITIVE DISCUSSION

Reminder: the objective of these lessons is to build interaction and role responsibility. "Mrs. Potter's Questions" is an effective tool to evaluate the process, not the product. The observer's reporting role is clarified with these 4 questions:

1. What were we expected to do?

2. What did we do well?

3. If we did the same task over, what would I/we do differently?

4. What help do we need?

CLOSURE

Provide opportunity for children to see the work of other groups. At the early stages of cooperative groups, keep the "product" simple but interesting...it is NOT the goal. Because children love to see what their friends did, do take time for a closure of sharing.

003
CHAPTER

Search for Somebody

BACKGROUND	To give students lots of practice in verbalizing their ideas and in gathering information from listening to others' ideas, we can structure activities that require them to interact with each other. The Search For Somebody or the People Search is such an activity. It is a generic strategy that can be used as a lesson focus, a review, or a transition.
	Recalling personal past experiences makes the search an especially rich strategy with many applications.
THINKING SKILL	Articulation and Active Listening
FOCUS ACTIVITY	Ask students to describe a time when they lost something and how they went about searching for the lost item. After several descriptions, tell them that they are going to go on a "search" today.
OBJECTIVE	To provide an opportunity for articulation and listening.
INPUT	Provide students with directions for the search either by telling them (non-readers) or giving them a copy of a search.

In this example, they will be searching for somebody who can help them with information about tadpoles and frogs (a transition activity into science time).

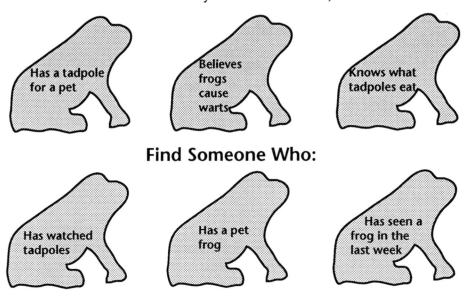

Find Someone Who:

ACTIVITY

Have students "search" for six different friends who can sign their name to the "search" by explaining, describing, or telling them about an item on the paper. (For non-readers, direct them to search for one person at a time, e.g. find someone who has a pet frog).

The search can be focused on any topic. From the following examples, you can create more searches to suit your needs.

Lesson Extension:
Find Someone Who:

METACOGNITIVE DISCUSSION

After the children have done the search, ask them to P.N.I. the activity. Ask the students to tell what they thought was positive about the activity, what was negative, and what was interesting. Record their ideas on the board.

POSITIVE (+)		(What did you like?)
NEGATIVE (-)		(What didn't you like?)
INTERESTING (?)		(What was interesting about the search?)

CLOSURE

Elicit ideas for a search students can do at home that night. Suggest that they try to think of questions or statements to use with the family (e.g., find somebody who likes the same TV show as you do).

Fat and Skinny Questions

BACKGROUND	Young children are bubbling over with an endless stream of questions as they explore the world about them. They are forever "gathering" data as they try to fit the pieces together into meaningful patterns. To emphasize the value we place on their "thoughtfulness," the mystery box is a motivating and appropriate activity.
THINKING SKILL	Questioning
FOCUS ACTIVITY	1. Have an object concealed in a box. Pass the box around the circle of children and have them use all their senses to "gather data" about the contents of the box. 2. Elicit "blind guesses" and record the ideas on a chart.
OBJECTIVE	To generate and evaluate student questions.
INPUT	Create a matrix (or grid) on the board. Tell the students that they are going to ask questions about the contents of the box and then rate the questions as either "fat" or "skinny" questions.

	Fat	Skinny
Is it a toy car?		X
Where would I find it?	X	
What shape is it?	X	
When might I use it?	X	

Explain that "fat" questions take up more space; they require "fat" answers that give more information than "skinny" questions that can be answered in one word, such as yes or no.

ACTIVITY

Have students talk with a partner about their ideas. Then as partners, they must decide on one "fat" question they want to ask about the contents of the box. They must be prepared to tell you why they think it is a "fat" question.

As students ask their questions, record them on the grid. From the questions, help students gather the facts about the mystery box until they know from the facts what is in the box. Then, of course, open the box and reveal the proof of their good questions and thinking.

METACOGNITIVE DISCUSSION

Probe them to decide if questions are "fat" or "skinny" and why they think so. Remind students that "fat" questions require more thinking than "skinny questions.

Record the marks on the grid as they decide.

CLOSURE

Using the stem: "Fat questions are like _____," have students describe their perceptions of "fat" questions.

Start Them Thinking Critically

Can Sally Tally?

BACKGROUND	One of the most useful skills we can teach children is how to organize data. While the quantity and availability of information continues to expand, we can share simple organizational strategies with very young children. If we do this early, as their base of knowledge increases and their need to organize more data expands, they will have had preparation for more sophisticated skills of organization.
THINKING SKILL	Organizing Information
FOCUS ACTIVITY	Use tallies to record the number of votes for favorite stories from the last week.
OBJECTIVE	To use the strategy of tallying to record and organize varied data both accurately and quickly.
INPUT	Demonstrate what a tally mark is by taking a simple vote. Example: Which show do you like better? Choose two current titles.

(TV SHOW #1)   (TV SHOW #2)

Tallying is often used in classrooms by teachers. Introduce it as a tool for children. Let them practice with the slash mark method (卅).

Ask, "Why do we tally?" Wait until you get the responses "accuracy" and "speed."

With tallying as an organizational tool, children can take votes; keep a running total; see relationships of pennies to nickels, nickels to dimes, and dimes to quarters; organize random data for graphing and other analysis; and keep accurate scores for partner games. It's simple...but valuable! Children five and six years old can learn, love, and use tallying.

ACTIVITY

Here are two thinking games using the strategy of tallying:
I. POISON
- for two players
- children can tally their wins without teacher involvement

Need: 12 similar items (such as white buttons, paper clips, pennies)
1 dissimilar item which is the "poison" on the score sheets

Rules: Take turns removing 1 or 2 items at a time. Person who must take the "poison" is the loser.

There is a pattern...find it and you will be a winner! Winner gets to make a tally mark on small 3" X 3" Tally Sheets. You can play to a certain total or to a time limit.

<u>POISON</u>

<u>ANN</u>	<u>JOE</u>
卅	//

II. SWITCHEROO

- one player
- child can tally each move...thus organizing his or her actions
- put coins on the pictures (2 pennies and 2 dimes)
- put the pennies where the dimes were and the dimes where the pennies were
- a move is a slide to another box or a jump over ONE coin
- when you make a move (slide or jump), record a tally mark. Object: Try to do it in 8 moves. There is a pattern. See if you can find it!

METACOGNITIVE DISCUSSION

On a 4" x 6" piece of paper, have children make a mark like this (/) anywhere on the paper every time you say "mark." Do this 20 to 30 times.

Now turn the paper over and have the children make a mark every time you say "mark." Remind them now to tally (*////*) (Ask..."What does that mean?"). Again, do it 20 to 30 times.

Ask them to tell you how many marks are on each side. Record the differences. Ask "Which way is more accurate? Why does one way give you the results faster?"

CLOSURE

Have children create an original picture from their tally sheets:

006
CHAPTER

A Handful of Coins

BACKGROUND

Reading bar graphs is a basic skill, and children have many opportunities to read these "information pictures." But how often are children expected to understand where the information (data) came from? Being able to read graphs is important, but when children become aware of applications for graphing and can put collected data into a meaningful graph then critical thinking (analysis and synthesis) occurs.

THINKING SKILL

Organizing Data for Analysis

FOCUS ACTIVITY

Tally the lunch count for the day on the board.

Hot   _____

Cold   _____

Go Home   _____

Absent   _____

OBJECTIVE

Plug data into a graph for analysis.

INPUT   (This is not an initial graphing lesson. Children need to have some graph reading experience.)

Pair children with a partner.

Draw one of these graphs on the board.

For Younger

	Penny 1¢	Nickel 5¢	Dime 10¢	Quarter 25¢
6				
5				
4				
3				
2				
1				

For Older

	1¢	5¢	10¢	25¢
12				
11				
10				
9				
8				
7				

Explain that each child has a responsibility: One partner will get a handful of coins from the teacher. The other partner will get 2 prepared graphs like the one on the board and 4 crayons or markers.

Ask how they can use what they have (coins, paper, markers) to make a graph.

What will they need to do first?

ACTIVITY

Observe/help children having problems by asking questions such as: "What are you supposed to show me in this first column? How do you figure out the number of sections to color?"

Share graphs. Compare/contrast between partners, then various individuals.

Students must be prepared to answer:

What does your graph show you?
What was your data today?
What did you do first?
Why is John's different from Jim's?
Looking at the graphs, who took the biggest handful? How do you know?

METACOGNITIVE DISCUSSION

Tomorrow, I could graph . . .

I would like to graph . . .

CLOSURE

With **young** children have them:

1. Put coins in rows or columns by attributes of size, color, or monetary value.

2. Count.

3. Examine heads and tails.

4. Make original patterns (pp, n, d, q, pp, n, d, q).

With **older** children have them:

1. Find totals for each bar or graph.

2. Find differences in value of "dime total" and "nickel total."

3. Find other ways to classify coins.

Clay Is More Than Play

BACKGROUND	Attribute identification is a cornerstone for thinking skills such as comparing and contrasting, categorizing, and classifying. The skill of identifying attributes requires practice before it becomes a useful tool. One well-planned lesson permits children to manipulate clay (great for small muscles), to create geometric solids (not just hear about them) and to reinforce one of the necessary skills of critical thinking: attribute identification.
THINKING SKILL	Attribute Identification
FOCUS ACTIVITY	Have students brainstorm words about clay as you give them a chunk of clay.
OBJECTIVE	To infuse attribute identification practice into both the math and art curriculum while encouraging small motor activity and vocabulary development.
INPUT	Clarify and define vocabulary: 　　attributes　　cube 　　sphere　　cone 　　cylinder

ACTIVITY

1. Present each child with a piece of modeling clay. You, as teacher, will also need clay.

2. Tell children to soften clay by squeezing while you share some new words with them. Say, repeat, and write on the board: sphere, cylinder, cube, cone (rectangular solid, if age-appropriate).

3. Ask each child to roll clay into a sphere. (You may have to demonstrate.) When they look at yours, and say "that's a ball," tell them a sphere is like a ball, and today we will learn the correct name—sphere.

4. Say: "Tell me something about your sphere." Accept comparisons to ball, sun, but work toward common identifying attributes such as: it has no flat sides, it rolls, it goes round and round, it's smooth, etc.

5. Using the word sphere, brainstorm a list of things shaped like a sphere.

6. Say, "Let's go add an attribute to our spheres today." (Example: poke two pencil holes in our clay spheres.) Depending on developmental age, you might say: "Our spheres have two pencil holes; do all spheres have to have holes? Why or Why not?"

7. Now put your clay sphere on the table and roll it into a cylinder...Not skinny like a snake, make it a fat cylinder. Now tap each end gently. (demonstrate) "What can you tell me about a cylinder? What do you see? Look at the ends. What are some attributes of a cylinder?"

8. Brainstorm lists of cylinder-shaped items.

9. Now make a sphere again. "Show me your spheres. We're going to make a cube. That's just like a box, a die, or a counting block. (Show items if children need visual clues.) If you tap the sides gently, you can make a cube (demonstrate).

10. Say, "Look carefully at your cube. What do you see? Let's count the sides. Can you name some attributes of a cube?"

11. Ask, "Do you see any cubes in our room?" Allow ample time for recognition, identification, and justifications.

METACOGNITIVE DISCUSSION

Let children choose a shape and make four practice shapes. As you move around the room, ask children: "Which shape did you make best? Why? What shape is the hardest to create? Why?" Have children group themselves by shapes; count and tally how many of each kind; name at least one attribute of a chosen shape; discuss why more "spheres" (if that's the case) and less "cubes" were made.

Note: In an activity like this, many children will identify by what the shape is not...that's O.K. If it's not flat, not a cylinder, and not egg-shaped...but it rolls...it just might be a sphere!

CLOSURE

Allow free time with clay. Some children will create more shapes and discuss attributes of their creations...even though they may be unaware of the process. Others may just want to create original non-descriptive sculpture.

Whose Shoes?

BACKGROUND	If children are to use the skills of comparing and contrasting, they must be able to identify attributes. By allowing children opportunities to use their senses, to observe and name attributes of a concrete item, an understanding of the word and its meaning materializes. Children need numerous opportunities to observe attributes, identify critical attributes, and tell how they found the attributes. A firm formation in attributing provides structure for other thinking skills such as classification and sequencing.
THINKING SKILL	Attribute Identification
FOCUS ACTIVITY	Ask students to list attributes to describe you (the teacher).
OBJECTIVE	To identify three observable attributes of a concrete item.
INPUT	With young children, sit in a circle and have each child remove one shoe. As teacher, use your shoe to model observation. Name three attributes of your shoe and explain which sense(s) were used. Example: "My shoe is gray, has one buckle, and feels rough. I found these attributes with my eyes and my hands." Then place the shoe in the center of the circle.

ACTIVITY	Proceed around the circle having children do the same.

METACOGNITIVE DISCUSSION	Say: "When I look at all those shoes in the center of the circle, I can find mine by..." "How could you find one more attribute using a different sense...?" (touch, smell, sound, taste, sight) "Remember the Old Lady Who Lived in the Shoe. I wonder how we might name attributes of that shoe." Concrete examples for older children: Use pencils, pens, or gym shoes.

CLOSURE	Have children keep the shoes they are still wearing hidden from view. "Who will volunteer to pick one shoe and give it to the correct owner? Shoe owners share three attributes of their shoe." Volunteers should then pick the correct shoe out of the pile. Have children take turns returning shoes to proper owners.

When You're In, You're In When You're Out, You're Out

BACKGROUND

A group is delineated as such because its members share at least one common or critical attribute. Once children are able to identify attributes through observation, they need practice in zeroing in on the critical attribute. This skill is a prerequisite for analyzing; for the organization of data; for the comparison of data; and for the judgment of data.

THINKING SKILL

Analyzing for Critical Attributes

FOCUS ACTIVITY

Show students a square and a circle. Ask for attributes. Ask for the attribute that is most important for distinguishing the two (straight, curved).

OBJECTIVE

To identify the critical attributes that identify members of a group or category.

INPUT

For young children, draw a simple but large house or box on chart paper or the chalkboard. For older children, draw any appropriate closed shape on chart paper or the chalkboard.

Explain that certain items (names/words/pictures — whichever you choose to begin) will be put in the house because they have at least one special attribute called a **critical attribute**. Other (items) will go out of the house. Ask if you need to make comparisons (and you do). For what do you have to look and how? If necessary, review how to find attributes.

ACTIVITY

Begin with a simple topic like "girls' names," "farm animals," or "4-wheeled vehicles."

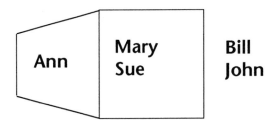

Continue to add items both in and out. When children name a common attribute but not a critical one for your pre-determined category, select a word for easy identification of why the suggested attribute won't work.
Example: Names that begin with J.

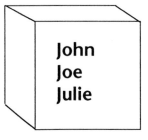

They say "boys," you say, "Tom goes out, Julie goes in."
As their skill improves (and you become adept at the activity)
increase the number of critical attributes.

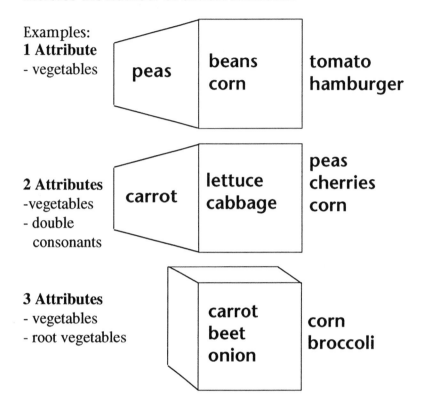

Examples:
1 Attribute
- vegetables

peas | beans corn | tomato hamburger

2 Attributes
-vegetables
- double
  consonants

carrot | lettuce cabbage | peas cherries corn

3 Attributes
- vegetables
- root vegetables

carrot beet onion | corn broccoli

This activity "plugs in" to skills across the curriculum. It can
be done daily in a few minutes for awareness of attributes,
group membership, and reinforcement of skills being taught.
The following is an accumulated list of various "plug-ins" for
classroom usage. Suggestion: as you use one or create a new
one, write it in curriculum manuals where appropriate. You
will amass a collection of valuable uses.

**METACOGNITIVE
DISCUSSION**

To find why certain things go in the house/box, I need to...
If color is not the attribute, I might look for...
If smell is not the attribute, I might look for...
If place is not the attribute, I might look for...
If size is not the attribute, I might look for...
If word sounds are not the attribute, I might look for...
If word structure is not the attribute, I might look for...

CLOSURE

After identifying the grouping or category of the house/box, close with a cumulative game where each person names something that would fit the day's group. It is cumulative because they repeat the previously named items. Example: Today's house was fruit from a tree.

1st person...apple

2nd person...apple, pear

3rd person...apple, pear, orange

When closing an activity with a cumulative wrap-around, children should understand they can "pass" if they cannot add to the list. Encourage descriptive words such as "Jonathan" apple. This allows for more additions to the group.

Path of Patterns

BACKGROUND Patterns are the essence of uniqueness. Discerning patterns of similarities and differences leads to the classification process. Classification precedes perceptual awareness of degrees of differences. Once these subtleties become apparent, sequential synthesis and abstract association can occur. Application of the resulting analogous relationships ushers ideas to the threshold of patterned uniqueness, the structure of all creativity. With patterned uniqueness, we create original designs in dance, music, art, literature, science, history, and ultimately life itself.

Structure of Creativity

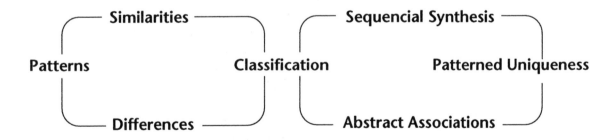

THINKING SKILL   Perceiving Patterns

FOCUS ACTIVITY   Observe, perceive patterns, seek structure, recognize relationships, and construct connections. Read this poem about
patterns to the students.

Wingborne
by Gwen Frostic

The lines of wind-blown sand on the dunes
...of the snow as it falls in beautiful drifts
the lines of the clouds
in the sky above...
and the water that washes upon the
sands...
forever and ever, these lines repeat...
always and always
each one is unique...

Dry leaves rise in a gust...
...tiny birds in little flocks...
gulls soar...
insects swarm...
seed whirl and sail...
millions of time as the formation repeats...
each time...each thing
unto itself is unique.........

All the stars on clear still night...
... all the leaves on a single tree...
the many ideas that one may have...
Over and over...
...the basic concept repeats...
Yet each star...
each leaf...
each idea...
each one is unique.........

OBJECTIVE   To investigate the patterns of nature and use observation
skills to group and classify.

INPUT

PATH OF PATTERNS: After reading the poem, initiate the unit by exploring a path of patterns. Nature provides a rich and diverse setting to elicit observations of similarities and differences. Using the sections of an egg carton, have students collect twelve samples of "patterned uniqueness" for further investigation back in the classroom. (For younger children, a study guide directing their observations might include leaves, rocks, trees, flowers, berries, apples, clover...)

ACTIVITY

There are four investigations that may take several days to complete. You will need to decide what is most appropriate for your situation.

Investigation 1: Comparing Collections

In small groups, analyze samples from the path of patterns walk by grouping and regrouping in smaller numbers of total sets. (For example, group all your samples in three sets and tell why.) Finally group all samples as a total class and brainstorm attributes considered for the mass groupings. Elicit further examples in nature of "patterned uniqueness." Discuss the need for categories and classification measures.

Investigation 2: Sort and Sequence

Combine all similar samples (all leaves, all rocks, etc.). Have small groups of students develop sequences for their sets. Criteria used in sequencing may include attributes of color, size, texture, substance, taste, smell, sound, frequency of occurrence, location.... Brainstorm other sequences and cycles in nature.

Investigation 3: Pea Pod Model

Distribute one specimen of a similar sample to each student (pea pod, maple leaf, acorn) and instruct him or her to "adopt it": look at it, examine it, get to know it while noting any distinguishing signs. Name it. After sufficient investigation, direct student to place his or her item into a pile with all the others. Scramble samples in the pile. Then ask students to reclaim their adopted items from the pile. (Each adopted item should be quickly found by its owner.) Following a discussion of patterned uniqueness, have students compare two peas in a pod, two maple leaves, or two acorns, using a Venn diagram:

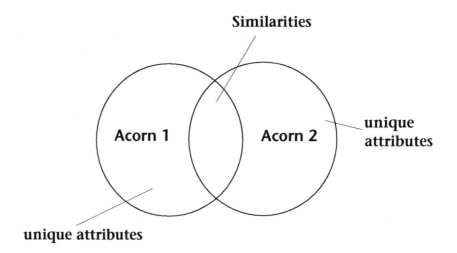

Investigation 4: Matrix Models

Using one set of samples (for example, leaves), demonstrate classification within a matrix.

	RED	YELLOW	GREEN
MAPLE			
OAK			
ELM			

Have partners develop similar models and explain their matrix models. Continue with matrix models until each group has designed several different ones. Be sure to have students investigate the diagonal of the matrix. Direct students to move row 1 to row 3, column 1 to column 2, etc. Note the diagonals each time. Matrix attributes could encompass color, size, shape, texture, smell, or sound. Discuss degrees of differences.

**METACOGNITIVE
DISCUSSION**

After working with several investigations, ask the students the questions of the "connecting elephants."

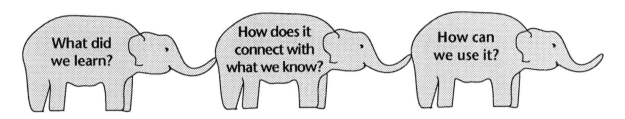

CLOSURE

Ask students to do a wrap-around using the lead-in: "I see patterns in _____."

When to Venn?

BACKGROUND	When students are able to observe, identify, and verbalize the attributes of a concrete object, they can work with more than one object and identify similarities and differences. Young children can become comfortable with the vocabulary and skill concepts by using their bodies, their clothes, and their friends—avoiding an overload of paper work and small motor demands.
THINKING SKILL	Comparing and Contrasting
FOCUS ACTIVITY	Use the teacher's chair and a student's chair. Ask how they are alike and how they are different.
OBJECTIVE	To verbally compare and contrast concrete items by naming the similarities and differences.
INPUT	Explore the concept of sets and Venn diagrams briefly.
ACTIVITY	Have all the girls stand up. Ask what is one common attribute of the group. Explain that a picture can be made showing the

attribute. It is called a "Venn Diagram." Draw a circle and
label it GIRLS as shown below.

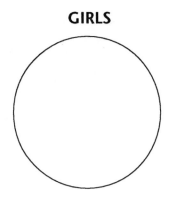

From the large group, make a sub-group of girls with tennis
shoes. Ask what the second common attribute is: draw and
label, TENNIS SHOES.

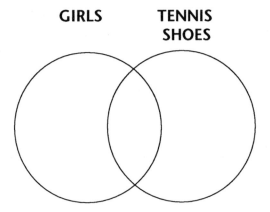

Using the concrete groups, go through each girl and place her
name in the section with only one attribute (GIRL) or with
two attributes (Girl/Tennis Shoes)

Use the term "intersection," emphasizing that it represents more than one attribute. If the skill of attribute identification has been mastered, the Venn diagram will help children comprehend the important dimension of visual comparison.

Depending on level of understanding ask: "Where can I put John (who has tennis shoes and is not a girl)?" Encourage children to identify these attributes (boy/tennis shoes).

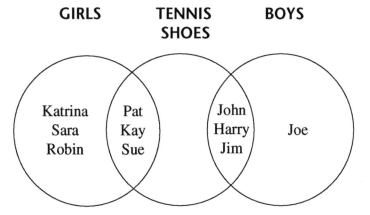

| GIRLS | TENNIS SHOES | BOYS |

| Katrina Sara Robin | Pat Kay Sue | John Harry Jim | Joe |

METACOGNITIVE DISCUSSION

For **young** children, have them draw some intersecting circles and color the intersections . . . have them draw squares and try to get an intersection.

For **older** children (Discuss or Log entry):
I think the hardest part of doing Venn diagrams is . . .
A Venn diagram helps me to . . .

CLOSURE

Delineate with chalk lines the three specific areas where children can stand in sets. As the teacher moves a few children and him- or herself into set A, set B or the intersection, ask for the similarities and differences...use clarifying questions to help them identify critical attributes.

Allow each child to determine where he or she will stand and why.
Example: **BOYS SWEATERS**

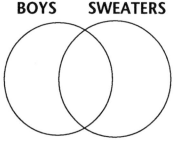

I Did a Grid

BACKGROUND

As children become more and more familiar with attribute identification, a logical move is to teach specific skills of comparing and contrasting. What better medium could we use with young children than books; classroom teachers read daily to children. Awareness of similarities and differences flows naturally with fiction and non-fiction literature. With careful planning and choice of shared books, children (even the youngest) will be able to use a grid of comparisons easily and effectively. The ability to write, the mastery of spelling, and the labor of sentence construction can all be eliminated—allowing time for mastering the critical skill of comparing and contrasting.

THINKING SKILL

Comparing and Contrasting

FOCUS ACTIVITY

Have students talk about how two of their favorite TV shows are alike and/or different.

OBJECTIVE

To identify attributes of both fiction and non-fiction books using a grid.

INPUT

1. Add a specific collection of 12 animal books to your classroom library. Choose 6 animals and select a fiction and non-fiction book for each. Examples:

   Timothy Turtle, by Al Graham

   The Turtle Book, by Mel Crawford

   the Story of Babar, by Jean DeBrunhoff

   Elephants, by Isobel Beard

   Danny and the Dinosaur, by Syd Hoff

   Giant Dinosaurs, by Erna Rowe

   These are only examples...consider using monkeys, dogs, cats, mice, rabbits, pandas, or even koalas.

2. Have a large grid on a bulletin board listing the names of the 12 books you will be using.

3. Place the animal book collection plus 10-15 additional books in the middle of a circled group of students. Ask what kind of a group or set it is. When identified as books, ask what attribute makes them books. With follow-up questions, arrive at the critical attribute of printed material in a "bound" form. (A printed newspaper is not a book. Older students should explore additional attributes of why a book is a book.)

4. Say: "Let's make some new groups. Who has an idea?" Ask children to suggest size, color, animals, etc..., have the books moved physically to a new group. Ask children to identify the critical attributes of a new group.

5. Be aware of the opportunity (if students are ready) to expose them to Venn diagrams without formal introduction. You can encircle both a "red group" and a "large size group" with chalk or yarn. The students may find difficulty in placing a large, red book. Use wait time (think time). Do not jump in with a solution too quickly. Go with the opportunity.

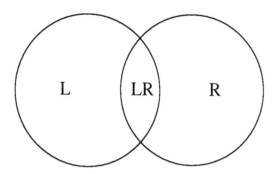

ACTIVITY

1. Read an age-appropriate non-fiction animal book. Identify both elements such as cover, title, title page, table of contents, pictures, and index. Explain that this is called a "non-fiction book" or an "information book." Ask,"Why is that a good name? What information did you learn? Did the book tell you something real or make-believe? Give me some examples." (Begin follow-up procedures described on next page.)

Book Title	Hard Cover	Soft Cover	Title Page	Table of Contents	Drawings	Photo-graphs	Animals Talking	Animals Not Talking
Timothy Turtle								

2. Show a fiction book about the same animal. First identify book elements and compare similarities and differences with the non-fiction book. Then read the book.

3. Discuss Content: "Is this real or make-believe? How do you know? What is one clue? Can you think of another clue? Let's look at the two books together" (most valuable when choosing non-fiction; look for books with actual photographs).

4. Each day read two books about one animal. The extentions are limitless depending on your writing and science curriculum. Teachers read to children every day; why not include critical thinking in the process?

Children can do their own grids to culminate a unit or to extend learning for those children who want to go "beyond" your curriculum.

Example:

Dinosaurs	Plant Eater	Meat Eater	4-legged	2-legged	Horned	Crested	Armored	Swimmer
Tyrannosaurus Rex								
Stegosaurus								

METACOGNITIVE DISCUSSION

For **young** children, include a parent involvement activity with the next home-bound library book.

Example:
We have been working on special kinds of attributes (characteristics of books). My teacher wants me to tell you three attributes about this book:

(1)

(2)

(3)

For **older** children who are keeping a Thinking Log, make a grid. (Do this as an explicit lesson. Math concepts are involved, so it's not wasted time.) Each day, thereafter, students will first write in the name of the shared book and check off attributes on their personal grids. Secondly, have students complete a statement.

Examples:
I think the most critical attribute of this book was

_____.

Today, of the two books I read, I preferred _____ because:

CLOSURE

(This activity should be done after each book discussion.) Using the large grid on the bulletin board, list the attributes identified. Try beginning with elements of a book and add fiction and non-fiction attributes. The first are easily identified, and the new skill of using a grid will not be confused with delineating content attributes. Have students work through each book, then use it as a wrap-up of discussion or, if necessary, as a guideline

Leave the Leaves to Us

BACKGROUND	Fall, the wonderful season when leaves turn to red, brown, green, yellow, and orange, and young children want to share each and every leaf they discover. For you see, theirs is the most beautiful leaf that ever was.
	Use these observations, the nature excitement, and the quantity of leaves to classify. The skill can be practiced by young children, especially when they gather the data.
THINKING SKILL	Classification
FOCUS ACTIVITY	Take a walk around school and collect leaves.
OBJECTIVE	To observe attributes of a large selection of leaves and to use this knowledge to list as many different categories as the children can identify. BEWARE: We, as teachers, tend to name categories and ask children to SORT! By doing this, we are thinking for them. We should let *them* name the categories for classification.
INPUT	Have a day designated as "Leaf Day." Explain that students should look for differences in leaves. Ask: "What makes leaves look different?"

ACTIVITY

Begin leaf activity by encouraging children to choose one very special leaf and name three attributes of the leaf. If this is their first experience with attribute identification, model carefully and encourage use of word "attribute". After everyone has shared, go to chart paper and explain: "We are going to observe all our leaves, pick out special attributes, and name a category. This means a special set/group/family."

Record: Sharp points

As you show them the leaf you were observing, let some children sort more leaves into this set, naming the attribute necessary for set membership.

Elicit net categories.

If children do not move beyond color and size, lead them with ideas to observing stems, veins, number of leaves on one stem, placement of leaves....

If children are ready, use a chalk Venn diagram on the floor with 2 or 3 attributes. Encourage verbalization of why they placed a leaf in a set or intersection.

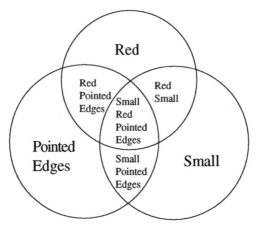

METACOGNITIVE DISCUSSION

My eyes helped me to classify because...
My fingers helped me to classify because...

The easiest group/set to find was...
The hardest group/set to find was...

CLOSURE

Choose 3-5 leaves from different categories/sets and make a crayon rubbing which clearly shows structural attributes of the leaves.

Pick Your Patterns

BACKGROUND

Patterns exist everywhere. Most of us are aware of obvious patterns in visual design and music. Those who see patterns, for example, in number systems, word structures, and linguistics, achieve at higher levels than those who see unrelated units. Time must be taken to teach, demonstrate, and practice patterning. If children don't naturally see patterns, that does not indicate they can't be taught to discover, see, and create patterns.

THINKING SKILL

Patterning

FOCUS ACTIVITY

Have students create a pattern with blocks.

OBJECTIVE

To use a simple grid to form and then discover varied patterns.

INPUT

Draw a sixteen-section, four-column grid on the chalkboard.

A	B	C	D
B	?		
C			
D			

Focus attention on the A, B, C, and D pattern in the top row and the first column. Ask children to tell you how many columns go down and how many rows go across. Explain that each row needs four letters...you can't have the same letter twice.

Ask a volunteer to decide what letter is going to go in the box with the question mark. Proceed down or across which ever way the child's thinking leads. Continue with another volunteer. If a mistake is made, have child look the row over and "tell what the problem is."

When grid is complete (see below), review each row across and each column down. This takes time, but teaching children to review and check their work is a skill. (Time taken early will pay dividends for years of learning.)

A	B	C	D
B	C	D	E
C	D	E	F
D	E	F	G

ACTIVITY

Draw a grid like the following one on the board. Ask children to look for a pattern. This is a practice skill for patterning. Children will already understand that a pattern is a form or configuration that has repetition or sequence.

Have volunteers identify and circle the patterns they find.

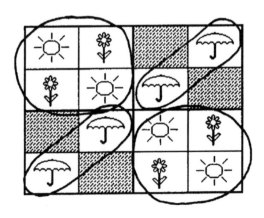

METACOGNITIVE DISCUSSION	Discussion: Look at what we did. What did we do first? Next?
	Who wants to share how you can check your grid?
	When you do your own grid, what do you need to know?
	Tell me about patterns in this grid.

CLOSURE	Have each child fold a piece of paper into 16 equal parts (a skill to be learned that is valuable for present activities and many future concepts).
	Depending on the age of the children, time of the year, curriculum, or the teacher's creativity, determine four new symbols and have the children set up their own grid. For the first few lessons go one line vertically and horizontally. The more comfortable children are with finding patterns, the more adventurous they will be in creating their own grids. When students are ready, increase grids to 25 and 36 parts.
	Have students share patterns. A colored crayon, pencil, or marker encourages the circling of additional patterns.

Can't Write, But Can Report

BACKGROUND	When confronted with a collection of data, a practical format will aid in showing relationships, marking comparisons and contrasts, and drawing inferences. Preparing reports can be effective, but for children they often demand writing skills that hinder organization and understanding of the content. If critical thinking is to be valued, it must provide a format which shows the data from which statements of analysis can be drawn or written.
THINKING SKILL	Reporting For Analysis
FOCUS ACTIVITY	Show them charts, graphs, and grids in their textbooks.
OBJECTIVE	Using a grid, children will list attributes, classify, and find relationships of multiple items having common attributes.
INPUT	Following are three examples for using a grid to accumulate report data in a format that promotes analysis and eliminates repetitive use of written reports. These grids can be done in a class, small cooperative groups, or individually for the anxious/curious learner. When subject and data is appropriate, consider using the grid as a teaching, testing, or practice tool.

ACTIVITY I

Children who are not yet proficient readers are capable of pursuing a collection of dinosaur books and reading or matching dinosaur names.

Teacher decisions: can they name attributes for grid? class? group? or individuals?

Dinosaurs	Plant Eater	Meat Eater	4-legged	2-legged	Duck-Billed	Crested (Bony)	Armored	Trassic Period	Jurassic Period	Creta-ceous Period
Tyrannosaurus Rex										
Stegosaurus										
Triceratops										

Questions for analysis: "What do the meat-eaters have that the plant eaters do not have? Why? Can you name two dinosaurs that have at least three of the same attributes?"

ACTIVITY II

When children work on sentence development and sentence structure, they can list multiple attributes of sentences. Using professionally published, teacher-prepared, or student-written sentences, fill in the grid.

Teacher decisions: Can children name *all* the attributes that you want identified? Is this a whole class activity for groups or individual work?

	Verb	Adverb	Noun	Pronoun	Adjective	Period	Question Mark	Comma	Quotes	Prep-osition
Sentence A										
Sentence B										
Sentence C										
Sentence D										

Questions for analysis: "Why are there so many checks in column one and so few in column two? Give me an example. Look at columns one and three. What do they tell you about sentences? Why does column eight give little information about the sentence?"

ACTIVITY III

When children study the 50 states, reports are usually written for each state. Perhaps analysis by comparing and contrasting and showing relationships of specific shared attributes would enhance the knowledge of the United States. Have children collect data to be plugged into a grid.

	North-east	South-east	Mid-west	North-west	South-west	Ocean Coastal	On Great Lakes	Land-locked	Pop. Over ___	Pop. Under ___

After collecting data, have reports written:

comparing Alaska/Alabama

comparing attributes of the Southwestern states

contrasting commerce in Coastal states and Inland states

METACOGNITIVE DISCUSSION

To record: When I make a grid, I need to _____

_____

When I look at the completed grid, I know _____

_____

CLOSURE

Brainstorm fruit. Brainstorm attributes of fruit. Group children and have them do a fruit data grid. (You might consider erasing brainstormed lists thus encouraging group input.)

Elves to Giants, Minnows to Whales

BACKGROUND

The skill of ordering is a critical skill for organizing data, ideas, and patterns. Size is only one way of ordering but much in our universe is dependent on size. Examples: elements of the food chain, sizes of food packaging, and featherweights to heavyweights in boxing. Awareness of size contributes to comparatives in "the big picture of knowledge."

THINKING SKILL

Ordering

FOCUS ACTIVITY

Place 3 students in front of the room. Ask someone to arrange them: tall, taller, tallest.

OBJECTIVE

To order, by size, a set of items that have a common attribute other than size.

INPUT

With young children, brainstorm a one-minute list of animals, a one-minute list of people they know, and a one-minute list of buildings.

	Animals	People	Buildings
Big			
Bigger			
Biggest			

Begin with reviewing the animal list and explaining that we need to find a big, bigger, and biggest animal.

Fill in the grid.

ACTIVITY

After doing the grid together, and if children are capable, have them work in groups and put each of the three one-minute lists in order. Compare group results.

Note: Depending on ability of children, you may not need to brainstorm idea lists first.

Suggestion:

	Animals	Fruits	Words	Classmates
Small				
Medium				
Big				
Bigger				

METACOGNITIVE DISCUSSION

Another way to order _____ is...

One way to order numbers is...
One way to order people is...
One way to order the 50 states is...

CLOSURE

Do a whip-around in which the first person names a huge animal or vehicle or fruit, and the next person must name a category item smaller than the previous, etc. Students have the right to pass when doing a whip-around. Return to those who passed and ask if they wish to add at this point.

Show the Flow

BACKGROUND

Sequencing. Putting in order. Often we fail to realize the great number of sequential patterns we live and deal with daily. From getting dressed, to starting a car, to writing a letter, to following a story plot, or to solving a problem, all are dependent on what happens first, second, and third. These procedures become automatic due to repetition. Young children need many opportunities to practice and understand sequential order. Too often, sequential activities rely on verbal activities only. Encouraging visual images where one sees the dependence of a relationship to a previous event helps children to understand how sequence plays an important role in our learning and living.

THINKING SKILL

Sequencing

FOCUS ACTIVITY

Cut out comic strips into individual frames and put the story back in order.

OBJECTIVE

To use a flow chart as a visual tool for teaching and practicing sequencing.

INPUT

This can be approached at least two different ways:

1. Share all the information and have children recall the sequence.

2. Suggest the end result and have children sequence the steps required to get there.

For the first experience in creating a flow chart, use a familiar story like *Jack and the Beanstalk*.

Draw a shape on the board and ask children what happened first in the story.

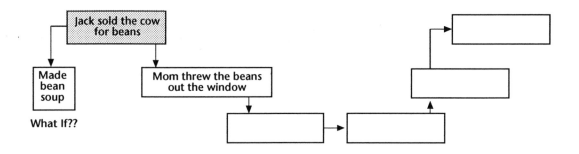

If they give information out of order, you may put it in the flow chart and let children discover the error as you review the sequence of a flow chart.

ACTIVITY

You need to turn in a book report. The last item on the chart is "I gave the teacher my book report."

Depending on ability and age, show how options can be shown on a flow chart. Even though you followed a certain path, alternatives might be suggested.

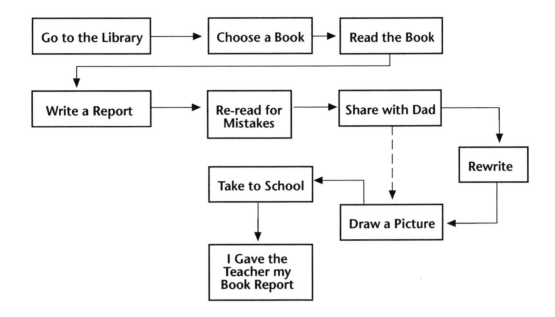

The flow chart strategy works well for problem solving. It offers a visual image for multiple options and provides a concise picture of sequence choices made.

METACOGNITIVE DISCUSSION

A flow chart reminds me of a _____.

I could make a flow chart for...

CLOSURE

Draw a large flow chart on the chalkboard and have the students record the activities of the day, class, or group.

Number One

BACKGROUND	Introduce young children to prioritizing and ranking for decision making. Life demands the skill! Children who experience numerous opportunities to rank and prioritize with metacognitive strategies for understanding included will be better equipped to make decisions about time management, entertainment choices, work obligations, and purchasing powers. Perhaps even the infinite number of multiple choice test questions to which they will be subjected will be less difficult!
THINKING SKILL	Prioritizing and Ranking
FOCUS ACTIVITY	Ask how many students are the oldest child in the family.
OBJECTIVE	To force children into making decisions by prioritizing, ranking, and analyzing.
INPUT	Depending on age and ability, these activities can be done orally in a large group, in small group activities, or individually.

Discuss the concept of "Number One" and explain that in this type of activity, there is no wrong answer. |

ACTIVITY

Ideas for initiating the skill, have students rank a group of items.

Explain: 1 is your first choice
          2 is your second choice
          3 is your third choice

Things to do:
____ go swimming   ____ wash dishes
____ go to an amusement park   ____ read a book
____ go horseback riding   ____ clean my bedroom

Things to eat:
____ fried worms   ____ broccoli
____ pigs feet   ____ peas
____ snake steak   ____ asparagus

I would rather be:
____ a King or Queen   ____ zoo animal
____ President   ____ farm animal
____ Astronaut   ____ jungle animal

Have some children tell *why* they ranked their #1 answer, and have some explain *why* they ranked their #3 choice.

Expose children to a concrete example of a Liekert Scale (a form of ranking). Begin with yes, maybe, no.

Continue to reinforce the importance of exploring why a choice was made and that there is no wrong answer.

Delineate an imaginary line with signs reading from left to right:

| YES | | MAYBE | | NO |

Make a statement and have children line up in front of one of the answers. Have each child give at least one reason for the position taken.

Examples:

The best hamburger is at _____.

A dog is the cleanest pet.

Multiplication is hard.

We should have inside recess today.

The "No Gum in School" rule is fair.

METACOGNITIVE DISCUSSION	Ranking and prioritizing might sound like "big" words but we do it quite often. Ask: "Tell me how you prioritize at the library? With your television? With your allowance? When is it the most difficult?"
CLOSURE	Give students three different fun activity papers or simple art projects. Tell them time permits them to do only one. Share reasons why they chose what they did (sometimes it is not a favorite, but the least unfavorite).

The Greatest, the Biggest, the Sweetest

BACKGROUND

Commercial television is here to stay. We can't "fight it" (and win) but we can join it—by using television commercials as a tool for critical thinking. Most children accept what they see and hear on TV as fact: "the biggest," "the sweetest," "the fastest." Children can learn to analyze exaggerations that occur regularly in TV commercials. This early analysis is the cornerstone for critical thinking skills of assumptions, inferences, bias, and propaganda. Young children can begin early, with guidance, to master these skills. Use the tool (television) with which they spend so much time.

THINKING SKILL

Analyzing for Bias and Exaggeration

FOCUS ACTIVITY

Show a photograph of a fisherman who has caught a small fish. Then tell a "fish story" about the fish as he might tell his friends. Ask how many know about "fish stories."

OBJECTIVE

By using a current television commercial, children will be able to identify words that make exaggerations and assumptions.

ACTIVITY	1. Choose a current commerical that is age appropriate and with which you can deal comfortably in your classroom. 2. Ask children to start looking for it on TV. 3. Discuss when they saw it. 4. Have children tell you what the commercial says or shows. Record their ideas. 5. Concentrate on the words or visual presentations of exaggeration and assumptions. With young children, keep it very simple. Call attention to words such as best, fastest, sweetest, everybody. Ask them to come up with even more words. Example Ad: You can now buy the best board game ever created—"Race Around the Track." It has 32 colorful, moveable cars with windows, wheels and drivers. Hurry, it's the best for any age—5 to 85! (Example: "the best." What does the word "best" mean?)
METACOGNITIVE DISCUSSION	With what game did you compare it? Who decides what "the best" game is? Why does "the best" differ? State, "Television tells us that this game is 'the best.' Those children that think 'Race Around the Track' is 'the best,' stand by the door. Those children that think that 'Race Around the Track' is not 'the best,' stand by the windows." Have children justify their reasons by positioning themselves. Allow children time to discover that "the best" is an exaggeration and an assumption made by the people who write the commercials and sell the products.
CLOSURE	Continue awareness of exaggeration words. Critical analysis for assumptions and bias depends on the basic identification of superlatives. This skill is a pre-requisite for analyzing for assumptions and bias.

Start Them Thinking Creatively

A Better Umbrella

BACKGROUND   Children have a wealth of ideas. In classrooms, time and numbers often limit the sharing and acknowledgement of these ideas. If we as teachers wrote into our lesson plans an activity called "That's a Good Idea" three times weekly, all children would have opportunities to listen, create, share, and be acknowledged as "thinkers." The applications of this activity are limited only by your planning. The idea of inventing a "Better Umbrella" is an introductory lesson to demonstrate the inventing process.

THINKING SKILL   Brainstorming

FOCUS ACTIVITY   Show students pictures of inventions. Vote on the best idea. Discuss inventing. Ask students to tell about some of their own inventions.

OBJECTIVE   To allow time for each child to be an active listener, to share an idea, and to receive a supportive comment from a class-mate.

INPUT   Arrange the class in a circle (sitting on the floor, on chairs, in desks, or standing). Explain that you as the teacher are going to add to this "thing" called an umbrella. Draw an umbrella on the chalkboard to make it more interesting and more helpful; or actually bring an open umbrella into the classroom to motivate student thinking.

ACTIVITY

You tell the person on your right an idea to add to the umbrella and that person must respond "That's a good idea because..." Then that person adds to the umbrella and tells his neighbor, who in turn responds "That's a good idea because..."

Each person should respond to the previous idea but may "Pass" if she or he cannot think of an addition to the umbrella.

Other ideas for "That's a Good Idea":
- Build a snowman
- Rearrange the classroom
- Plan the lunch menu
- Improve the school bus
- Solve a classroom problem

METACOGNITIVE DISCUSSION

Today, you had to do three things:
1. Listen.

2. Think of a reason why your neighbor's ideas were good ones.

3. Think of a new idea yourself.

Which was the easiest? Why?
Which was the hardest? Why?

CLOSURE

Have each student draw this new creation called an "umbrella." If students are older, have them draw the umbrella, and write a TV ad trying to sell the new "product."

Let's Go Piggybacking

BACKGROUND	The more ideas, the better the solution. When observing children (or adults) brainstorming, you will observe the skill of "piggybacking." When an idea is offered, it triggers a relationship in someone's thinking, and a new idea emerges immediately. Not all participants see or make those relationships, but that doesn't mean they can't learn how to "piggyback."
THINKING SKILL	Finding Relationships
FOCUS ACTIVITY	Ask how many kids have had a piggyback ride. Have them explain it and use other words (like "hooking up") to describe it.
OBJECTIVE	To demonstrate several ways of making relationships so one idea can spark additional ideas.
INPUT	Focus on an earlier brainstorming list using the idea of piggybacking. Count the number of ideas recorded. Explain that we can add more ideas by piggybacking on the ideas we already have posted. (Young children may need a literal explanation of "piggyback.")

Example: Using a list of animals

If age appropriate, talk about animal names that rhyme (hog, frog) or types of dogs (Cocker Spaniel, Doberman, etc.)

> ### Animals
>
> cat   giraffe
> dog   horse
> mouse

Ask: What other animals are related to the cat? (lion, tiger...)

Now try "Horse." Any ideas?

ACTIVITY

Using a list of B____ words:

What endings could you add to bug to make more ballbugwords? (bugs, bugging, bugged)

Now try "bike."

> ### B____ Words
>
> ball   bug
> book   bike

Using a list of Action words:

> ### Action Words
>
> run   dive
> jump   hide
> smell   roll

> ### Ways to Use a Newspaper
> Read
> Wrap the garbage
> Line the birdcage
> Cover a window

What other actions does your nose do?
What else could you wrap?
When you dive into a pool, what other words do you think of? (swim, splash, float)

Some children naturally piggyback. Teach those who do not. Awareness of ways to piggyback lays groundwork for SCAMPER (Osborne's steps for brainstorming and problem solving).

METACOGNITIVE DISCUSSION	Have children dictate ideas and examples on a language experience chart entitled "How We Can Piggyback Ideas."
CLOSURE	Explain that you are going to say a word or an idea and if anyone can piggyback on this word/idea, he or she should just stand up and smile. Example: pencil, swim, laugh, or monkey.

A Storm of Ideas

BACKGROUND	Brainstorming ranks high as both a skill and a strategy to encourage divergent production. Many opportunities for divergent thinking occur in classrooms. When introduced early and practiced with young children, fluency and flexibility of ideas abound. They love to share and have many ideas. Experience charts have proven to be a valuable early reading vehicle. Record ideas on chart paper.
THINKING SKILL	Brainstorming
FOCUS ACTIVITY	Ask how many students have been to the Pachyderm House at the zoo.
OBJECTIVE	To encourage divergent production in a risk-free atmosphere.
INPUT	Focus the students' attention on a new, interesting word (perhaps related to your curriculum or to a special story or book). Record the word on chart paper, pronounce it, and have children play around with the phonetic sound and the visual letters. Ask them to share their ideas about what the word might be or might mean.

Example:
❑   Marrow (to introduce a skeletal unit)
❑   Aphid (to introduce insects)

ACTIVITY

1. Record all ideas.

2. Review list.

3. Send a copy home. (This encourages parent involvement and stimulates a high interest level for your planned activity, book, or curriculum.)

METACOGNITIVE DISCUSSION

I like to brainstorm because...
When we brainstormed today, I liked the idea...
I wonder how many...

CLOSURE

After reviewing a brainstorming list, post it in the room and use it for curriculum skills.

Example: Color the vowels yellow
            Circle the three-syllable words
            Choose one word and name some rhyming words

Children see their ideas become written words used over and over in the classroom. For beginning readers, this is very valuable. For the accomplished reader, skills become more meaningful when applied to material which students helped to create.

I'm an Expert

BACKGROUND

We've all heard the adage, "Write about what you know," and it sounds almost silly. How could we possibly write about something we do not know. Writing, after all, is the "inking" of our thinking. But sometimes we need to prime the pump for student writing. Students know about a lot of things. In fact, they are even "expert" at some things. Through brainstorming, we can focus students' thinking on their areas of expertise. Identifying the "expert" areas facilitates the writing process. Students are able to generate a first draft easily because they already have an abundance of information; after all, they are the experts.

THINKING SKILL

Brainstorming

FOCUS ACTIVITY

1. Ask students for synonyms of the word "expert."

2. Define the term "expert": Anyone *in this room* that knows more about a topic than any other person *in this room* is an "expert" on that topic.

OBJECTIVE

To generate personally meaningful writing ideas in the pre-writing stage.

INPUT

Model "I'm An Expert" with three areas of expertise and your supporting rationale:

I'm An Expert on...

a) *tree houses*, because I built seventeen tree houses while I was growing up. I know how to build them, where to build them, and where *not* to build them.

b) *ballet*, because I took ballet lessons for twelve years and I was in a real ballet company.

c) *horses*, because I had my own horse named Patches and I spent lots of time with him.

ACTIVITY

1. Ask students to privately list *three areas* of expertise, keeping in mind the operational (classroom) definition of the term "expert." Allow them time to think.

2. Using paired-partners, have students share one of their "expert" roles.

3. Then, have the students select one area of expertise and place a focus word in a small circle in the center of a sheet of paper.

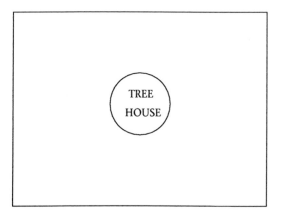

4. Instruct students to brainstorm with the focus idea by generating as many related words as they can. Demonstrate the "cluster" technique.

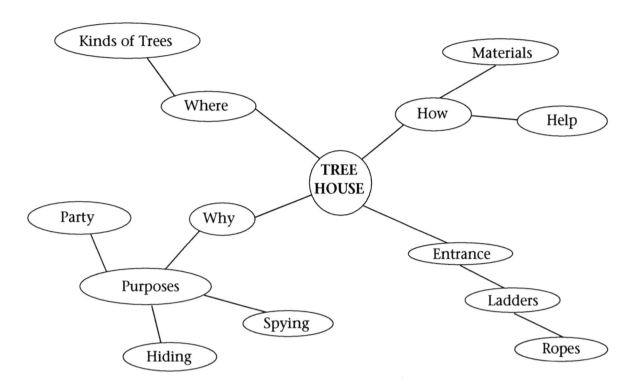

5. This may be done on a one-to-one basis for children learning to write, or used as an oral language exercise (without any writing), or modeled on the board for the entire group.

**METACOGNITIVE
DISCUSSION**

When we brainstormed today, I liked the idea...
Process the activity with a P.N.I. chart on the board.

POSITIVE (+)	
NEGATIVE (–)	
INTERESTING (?)	

CLOSURE

Make a LOG entry:

Brainstorming is like a "storm" in my brain because

_____.

Care, Feeding, and Training of a Pet Thesaurus

BACKGROUND

Through a whimsical story introduction, young children are invited to become familiar with the format and uses of a thesaurus (Junior version). Children will then have an invaluable tool to weave the tapestry of their work as they engage in the writing process.

The focus activity presents the mystery of the imaginary thesaurus to arouse children's curiosity and set the stage for the introduction of the reference book.

THINKING SKILL

Generating Synonyms

FOCUS ACTIVITY

Have you ever met a giant (or a pocket-sized) Thesaurus? I think it's related to the Brontosaurus or perhaps it is a distant cousin of Tyrannosaurus Rex. But it's not extinct! In fact, it's very much alive and is a true friend of humans. Some people even keep one as a pet right in the home. Often schools adopt a Thesaurus of their very own. There might be one right in our classroom; teachers seem to have a special fondness for a Thesaurus!

Use your imaginations and picture this mysterious Thesaurus. Is it thick? Colorful? Serious? Noisy? Humorous? Thoughtful? Enormous? Complicated? Talented? Smelly? Friendly? Creative?

As a pet, a Thesaurus is easy to care for. Really! It's no trouble at all. It doesn't even shed, and it eats practically nothing. It sits quietly in any corner until you coax it out, gently, with a few appropriate words. Then it responds in ways beyond your wildest imagination.

After reading the story, ask children to draw their versions of a "Thesaurus." Invite discussion of their ideas and why they think their interpretations are reasonable.

OBJECTIVE

To generate ideas through use of a thesaurus.

INPUT

After sharing the illustrations, dramatically reveal the pet Thesauruses hidden in the closet. Allow time for them to explore the books and elicit descriptions and information from them. Develop a class definition of a thesaurus. Instruct children in the use of a thesaurus. Have the children think first of several words in their heads and then find them in the thesaurus.

ACTIVITY

Apply the students' new research skills through a clever elaboration of school rules. The final products make colorful and intriguing displays throughout the classroom or school building.

Model one with the class. Then allow time for children to brainstorm a list of verbs that are often used in school rules. Using colorful poster board, have students produce "Real and Righteous Rules for Schools." For example:

Do not YELL... SCREAM, SCREECH, SHRIEK, SHOUT, BELLOW, WHOOP, YAMMER, YAP, CRY, CHEER, SQUAWK, CLAMMOR, ROAR, BAWL, BARK, OR HOWL... in the classroom.	Do not THROW... EJECT, CAST, PITCH, FLIP, CHUCK, LOB, PELT, STONE, PEPPER, VOLLEY, BANDY, TOSS, SLING, JERK, OR LAUNCH... food in the classroom.	THINK... REFLECT, STUDY, CONSIDER, DEBATE, REASON, MEDITATE, CONCLUDE, SPECULATE, PONDER, PUZZLE, MULL, THEORIZE, DELIBERATE, COGITATE, OR WONDER... about something before you speak out.

(You might duplicate the story of the pet thesaurus and send it home with the children to encourage parents to provide students with their own Junior Thesauruses.)

METACOGNITIVE DISCUSSION

1. Explain what a thesaurus is in your words.

2. Why is a thesaurus like a pet?

3. How is a thesaurus different from a dictionary?

CLOSURE

Complete this analogy in your log:

A thesaurus is like a dinosaur because both _____ .

Start With Me
(Mapping Everyone)

BACKGROUND	Skills to organize data...we can't teach too many of these or teach them too often! The vast quantity of information and knowledge published necessitates a ready supply of strategy tools to manage the data. The more practice young children have with beginning skills of organization, the more sophisticated will be their capabilities when "information overload" strikes!
THINKING SKILL	Organizing Information
FOCUS ACTIVITY	Show them several maps (of your state or city, for example).
OBJECTIVE	To create a "mapping" which will identify key words and show relationships of data.
INPUT	Introduce "mapping" with yourself (the teacher) as the subject. Children will be interested, and the mapped relationships will be meaningful.
	Draw a closed shape (be as original as you wish) on chart paper. Explain that you are going to map yourself. The vocabulary needed for understanding:

1. Key Words

2. Data (Information)

3. Relationships

4. Descriptors

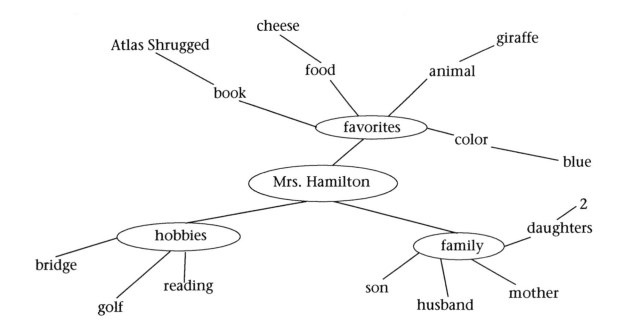

ACTIVITY

Start with a key word such as "hobbies." Your map can look like this ＼⌒ or this ⟋ or this ⌒♡⌒

Ask why "hobbies" is called a "key word." This is not an easy concept, but it is imperative to work on the concept and use the vocabulary if you want to develop mapping as an organizational tool.

Continue: Family
                Friends
                Favorites
                Schools

When you have supplied considerable data, ask if there is anything the children would like to know. If the information relates to a key word, have children tell you which one and why. If unrelated, map a new key word.

IMPORTANT: Explain that a mapping is never finished. Expand the map. Depending on the developmental level of the children, add descriptors.

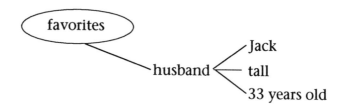

METACOGNITIVE DISCUSSION

Ask children to name and explain the four vocabulary words essential to developing and understanding mapping.

(Key Words) Have children identify key words on the mapping by highlighting them with a yellow crayon or highlighting marker. (A valuable practice—key words are the "meat and potatoes" to quality mapping. Consider requiring yellow highlighting on all mappings.)

(Data) Have children explain from where data comes.

(Relationships) Have children explain how the mapping shows relationships.

(Descriptors) Have children identify descriptors and tell how they relate to the rest of the map.

CLOSURE

Have children map themselves. Even young ones can draw pictures after you help put in key words. Children may choose the same key words used in the modeled lesson. That's okay for the first experience. However, encourage students to think of new key words. You might want to brainstorm a list of new key words with the entire class first.

Extensions: (Model new applications)
Stories from basal readers	State
Book reports	Class party
School building	Class zoo trip
Community	Creative writing

Writing Is Idea Sharing

BACKGROUND

A Faulkner novel or an O. Henry short story doesn't just happen! Time, opportunities to write, and encouragement are foundations from which quality writing grows. Often, teachers expect children to write too much, too well, and too rarely. Begin creative writing early and often with children. Help them, teach them, and fill their minds with shared ideas, descriptive words, and visual pictures *before* their words are dictated or written. Two or three descriptive phrases or sentences written daily will lead to paragraphs, short stories, and essays of quality.

THINKING SKILL

Generating Ideas

FOCUS ACTIVITY

Story, Filmstrip, Field Trip

OBJECTIVE

To implement a visual tool students can use to encourage fluency and freedom in creative thought and writing.

INPUT

Pre-Writing Instructions:

1. On chart paper, which should remain posted, make five columns. When there is a classroom lull, do a quick brainstorming activity for column 1. Example: Circus Animals.

Try to get 15-20 animals on the grid. Continue the other columns when convenient. This is the type of activity that can be done in a language arts period, or over a span of 2-3 days. It depends on your class and your scheduling.

Circus Animals	Circus People	Things to See Not Animals or People	Food/Drinks at the Circus	Who Goes?
Elephant Lion Pony	Trapeze Man Ring Master Lion Tamer	Whip Hoop Drums	Peanuts Pepsi	Mom Grandpa Me

2. Give children a large (12" X 18") piece of drawing paper. Review Column 1 and ask children to copy the names of three animals about which they could write. Proceed to Column 2 and choose three acts. Continue until children have 15 subjects on the paper.

3. When the schedule permits or art time arrives, have children review their list and draw a circus picture which has all 15 chosen ideas in it. Allow adequate time to draw. Remind children they must include all 15 things they chose. One question usually occurs: "Can I put something else in the picture?" The inspiration of sharing many, many ideas is at work!!

4. Have children share their picture with a neighbor, and if they can read, check to be sure all the ideas are included in the picture.

ACTIVITY

Now, have children do a creative writing. This can be done individually as children are drawing—a sentence here, a sentence there. Older children can write stories or poems.

Stories will usually be richer and more in-depth because children will have spoken and seen many ideas.

Bonus: many of the words they use will be pre-spelled on the five-column grid which remains visible in the room during the activity.

METACOGNITIVE DISCUSSION

For grid activity:

Tell me three ways this thing called a "grid" helps us for thinking and writing?

If we wanted a Column 6, we could add _____.

CLOSURE

Use one of the columns. Draw a line in front of the noun and have a wrap-around where each child gives you a descriptive word to be added to the grid list. (It might be color, size, or attitude.) In wrap-arounds, children have the right to pass if they cannot think of a word.

Examples:
Enormous Elephant   *Happy* Mom
Mean Lion   *Tired* Grandpa
Prancing Pony   *Excited* Me

White Out

BACKGROUND

To visualize in the mind's eye is to "see" images: when the characters come to life as colorful personalities; when the action grabs us emotionally; when we "know" the setting as a real place. Only then is reading really reading. To help young people process text for meaning, we need to provide practice in this skill of visualization. A good beginning is to first have students *recall* through visualization techniques, scenes and objects that are familiar to them already.

THINKING SKILL

Visualization

FOCUS ACTIVITY

1. Ask students to visualize their bedrooms. Then ask them to visualize the bedroom door. Does the door open into the room or out into the hall?

2. Ask students to visualize a penny. Which way is Lincoln facing?

3. Ask students to visualize getting dressed in the morning. Do they put the right or left sock on first?

4. Ask students to visualize the cereal cupboard and describe what they see on the shelf.

OBJECTIVE   To practice the skill of visualization.

INPUT   Using an overhead projector, place on the screen several
                             puzzle pieces from a large wooden puzzle that forms a shape
                             when solved: a horse, car, etc. Ask students to visualize the
                             puzzle completed and to *guess* what it is.

                             Discuss *how* they made their predictions and *why* they
                             guessed as they did.

ACTIVITY   Prepare overhead transparencies by "whiting out," using
                             typewriter correction fluid, black and white photographs,
                             drawings, or words:

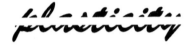   

                             Show the transparencies on the screen and elicit answers
                             from the students. Explain that the brain will fill in the
                             "missing parts" as it seeks familiar patterns. Provide many
                             variations of these visualizations using common words and
                             objects.

                             Then have students visualize transformations by reproducing
                             this picture on a transparency:

First show the picture one way. Have students "click a picture with their cranial cameras." Then invert the image on the screen. After a few seconds, turn off the projector and instruct students to *draw* the first image they saw. Compare their drawings to the overhead transparency in its original position.

On another day, warm up with "white out" exercises and then try another transformation.

METACOGNITIVE DISCUSSION

Discuss the following:

1. How visualization helps you recall and remember.
2. How visualization helps you "see" the characters of a story.
3. How seeing patterns is like _____.

CLOSURE

Make a LOG entry comparing how seeing patterns is like a

_____.

(game)

Edible Estimating

BACKGROUND

We estimate frequently in our daily lives:
    how many minutes to complete a specific chore
    how much pasta for six "big" eaters
    how far to the pond guarding the golf green
    how many "decorator marbles" to fill the crystal vase
        from Grandmother

The skill, when performed with acceptable accuracy, has been learned through experience and evaluation of the results. We do it naturally, sometimes without an analysis of our judgments. Starting children young will improve adult performance.

THINKING SKILL

Estimating

FOCUS ACTIVITY

Have the students estimate how many jelly beans are in a jar.

OBJECTIVE

Children will make and record measurement estimations to be compared with actual measurements and followed up with evaluative discussion.

INPUT	Read *The Littlest Rabbit* by Robert Krauz.

ACTIVITY (PART I)	Prepare or have children prepare a large quantity of simple paper carrots of two sizes (about 4" and 10").

On chart paper record each child's estimate of "how many long carrots tall" he or she is. (Use the word "estimate" and teach that estimates are educated guesses made from observing and making comparisons.)

HOW MANY BIG CARROTS TALL?

	Estimate	Actual
Karen	14	4+
John	6	4
Mary	9	3+

Depending on age level, class size, and time limitations, have children measure as a class, in groups, or with a partner and record actual measurements.

METACOGNITIVE DISCUSSION (I)	Review chart and ask which measurements were closest to the estimates. Ask the students to tell a partner how they made their estimates.

ACTIVITY (PART II)	Repeat activity using the 4" carrot.

HOW MANY SMALL CARROTS TALL?

Estimate	Actual
_____	_____
_____	_____
_____	_____

METACOGNITIVE DISCUSSION (II)

Have children circle or name the estimations that were good and tell why. Ask them to discuss differences in number of carrots tall when using two different size carrots.

Encourage each child to place a "+" or "-" by his or her estimation and explain why. If the lesson has been taught in a non-threatening climate, children will feel comfortable evaluating their estimates.

CLOSURE

Pass out real carrots. Have children estimate how many inches or centimeters (depending on where you are in the math curriculum) long their carrots are before eating! Wash or peel and EAT!

EXTENSION: *The Popcorn Dragon* by Jane Thayer. Estimate how many pieces of popcorn there are in a small paper cup, a large styrofoam cup, a lunch box, a drawer, a refrigerator— have fun!

I Predict . . .

BACKGROUND	What do you think will...? Children profit from numerous opportunities to make predictions. Young children need to be alert to multiple possibilities and to take risks when making a prediction. Most elementary classroom teachers encourage outcome predictions and possibilities for basal readers and shared literature. However, involving students with predictions directly related to their surroundings, their activities, and their families prepares them for everyday decision making. Two types of activities help to develop predictive skills. One: to predict what people will say, choose, or do ("soft" prediction). Two: to predict how many, what size, what time—observable, countable results ("hard" prediction). Children benefit from both types as well as from the traditional predicting of story results and endings.
THINKING SKILL	Prediction
FOCUS ACTIVITY	For a prediction activity choose an age appropriate idea, something with which all the children are familiar and which would be motivationally interesting to them. A favorite item in a specified group usually sparks personal interest and curiosity.
	Examples: favorite color, food, animal, TV show, ice cream flavor, singer, fairy tale, folk hero, outdoor sport, individual sport, athletes ("soft" predictions of "soft" data).

Examples: How many cars pass your house between 4:00 p.m. and 8:00 p.m., how many blue cars in the parking lot, how many pages in a book, how many commercials during a half-hour TV program ("hard" predictions of "hard" data).

OBJECTIVE

To make individual predictions and then gather information to compare the prediction with the outcome.

INPUT

One definition of "prediction" is anticipating what comes next. Synonyms are forecasting, guessing, and anticipating. (Have students use the thesaurus to find synonyms.) Examples: predicting weather, trends, or outcomes.

How to use: **B**ase on facts.
Examine probabilities and possibilities from clues.
Tender your best; take a guess.

ACTIVITY

1. Depending on age and ability of children, determine what the prediction activity will be. You may wish to determine the first one for a model and encourage their ideas when they understand the task.

2. Practicing the guidelines of informal brainstorming, record possibilities for the given subject prediction.

3. Discuss the word "predict" using synonyms (guess, forecast).

4. Discuss reasons why a specific show, food, or book is considered a favorite.

5. Have each child predict what they think will be the outcome. (If old enough, have children record in a Log, write on a piece of paper, or tell you. Save the predictions.)

6. Proceed with collecting information. This can be an oral activity or used as a mini-research activity which encompasses other critical skills of data collecting and bias-analysis.

METACOGNITIVE DISCUSSION

When I make a prediction I...

It's easy to predict_____, because...

It's hard to predict_____, because...

CLOSURE

On chart paper, record each prediction encouraging an explanation why each child made his prediction.

Ask children how they will find out if their prediction was correct. (The temptation is to explain that we collect data or take a survey. But wait until the children say "We have to ask, or look, or whatever. Let them do the thinking of how to accomplish the task!)

Become the Thing

BACKGROUND

If you have ever asked students to pretend they are a pencil in a desk and to imagine what it feels like, you have used the second level of analogy in Gordon's Synectics Model, the level called "Personification." In essence, the student "becomes the thing" and takes on the actions and feelings of that thing.

By giving students experiences with personification, we expose them to the idea of empathetic feeling that is necessary to understand other people. This technique also helps us imagine other situations and to try to reason by analogy.

THINKING SKILL

Personification

FOCUS ACTIVITY

Personal analogies: Using a simple transparency on the overhead projector, have students warm up by outlining "the thing" on notebook paper. The response, which must include actions and feelings, is then written within the outlined sketch.

For example:

Transparency

Student Response

I am a truck
leaving
town

Have them verbally tell a partner their actions and feeling as if they actually were the truck.

OBJECTIVE	To compare through the use of personification.

INPUT

Personal Analogy: Becoming the Thing

In personal analogy, the student involves himself, both emotionally and kinesthetically, in empathetic identification with the thing.

a. Action - Example: I am a tire bumping along.

b. Feelings - Example: I am dizzy from my spinning existence.

ACTIVITY

Using some of these suggestions, lead students into writing their ideas. Each piece must contain the *actions* and *feelings* of the object. They must become the object and write from that point of view.

1. Animate Things: I am a: caterpillar, fish, evergreen tree, eagle, alien.

2. Inanimate Things: I am a: telephone, robot, soap bubble, ladder, pair of roller skates.

**METACOGNITIVE
DISCUSSION**

Discuss what was interesting about doing the personification. Ask if it was easier to pretend to be an animate or inanimate thing. Discuss why that might be.

CLOSURE

Use a wrap-around with this lead-in:

I like to use my imagination because...

You're "In Fer" a Big Surprise

BACKGROUND

Observing and inferring are two critical thinking skills. Like two peas in a pod, they are closely related, but distinctly separate. Children make observations. Children make inferences. However, not enough time is spent emphasizing the differences between observing and inferring. Children will benefit from many, many experiences using the two skills together in relation to the phsyical world. The transition to implied inferences in both reading and conversation will materialize naturally when children have recognized, recorded, and compared their observations with their inferences.

In this lesson, you will set up student observations and "hook em" with a surprise. By frequent comparisons of the two critical skills, the ability to recognize inferences (which is difficult for many students) will improve.

THINKING SKILL

Inferring

FOCUS ACTIVITY

Stand with your hands crossed, looking stern. Ask the kids what they can tell about your mood. Talk about body language and facial expression. Have them try some.

OBJECTIVE	To demonstrate and record the differences between observations and inferences using familiar items in the physical world.

INPUT	Put the word "observation" on the chalkboard. Ask who knows what it means. Elicit ways to do it. The use of all the senses is crucial to observations, not just the eyes!

ACTIVITY	After discussion of the word, record children's observations of you...

Examples: You have a red dress.
               You have black hair.
               Your earrings are gold.
               You are happy.
               You can't see too well.
               You are a nice teacher.

When they contribute an inference statement rather than an observation, record it by putting an "*" in front of it.

Review the list and call attention to the statements of inference. Tell children you need a new list for things that are not observations. They are called "inferences."

Put the inference statements under "inferences." Ask if they know the difference. Remember, if they knew and understood the differences, we wouldn't have to teach it. Lead them to understand that when they can actually see, touch, hear, smell, or taste something, it is an observation. Inferences are ideas we get from clues or experiences we have had.

Say, "Now let's try again."

Show one side of a shiny, red apple (keeping a badly bruised, seedless, or coreless side hidden). Ask for observations about the apple.

Record: Observations

Example: Red
              Juicy
              Good
              Seed

Show the apple. Now ask, "Which ideas are inferences? Why? Can we add more observations and more inferences to our list?"

Other ideas: Show a ball point pen (no insides).
              Show a book (one with nothing written inside).
              Show a stapler (no staples).
              Show pictures of a person in a car (going where, or not going?)
              Show a dog.

METACOGNITIVE DISCUSSION

Discussion: One difference between an observation and an inference is...

I think it is easier to make an _____ because...

CLOSURE

Ask children what inferences they might make as you make the following statements (allow time to think).

Look at those dark clouds.
I'm going to put a sweater on.
Look at the buds on that tree.
.I have to take my shoe off quickly.
Take your crayons out of your desk, please.
There's frost on the window.
That robin sits all day on the nest.
The gym teacher is outside with a net and a volleyball.

The Big Idea

BACKGROUND

Sidney Parnes, one of the founders of the creative problem-solving model, suggests in his book *Aha!* that we ask students at the end of a learning session to: (1) state the big idea; (2) think about how that idea *connects* to what they already know; and (3) think about how they might *use* that new idea or connection. He goes on to say that by capturing the concepts this way, we can propel student thinking to new levels of understanding and meaning.

THINKING SKILL

Generalizing

FOCUS ACTIVITY

1. Before class, tell two students who are about the same height to stage two arguments in front of the class. They are to argue about which one of them is taller.

2. In the first scene, they will argue and finally resort to pushing and shoving each other, leaving the scene mad and upset.

3. After a brief break, they will re-stage the argument scene. This time they will argue and then agree to accept the verdict of an outside party. Then they will ask someone to actually measure them. They will leave on friendly terms with the argument settled to the satisfaction of both people.

| **OBJECTIVE** | To elicit generalizations from students as they process information. |

INPUT	1. Using the image of an elephant (see next page), introduce the concept of the "big idea." Ask them to discuss the two episodes with a partner and try to decide what the big idea was in each scene. Elicit sample responses after they have discussed it (e.g., an argument about size).
	2. Lead them beyond the concept of "main idea" to the concept of "generalization" or "lesson" that they see as they consider both scenes. Elicit examples from their experiences that are similar to help them connect (e.g., one can solve arguments in two ways—violent or non-violent).
	3. Then ask them to tell their partners how they can use the generalization in the future.

| **ACTIVITY** | To symbolize the "big idea," read a book or show a film about friendship or fear or a similar concept. Afterward, have them draw their "big idea" inside the elephant on the next page. |
| | NOTE: It will take many short practices for young students to see beyond the main idea to generalization—but with skillful probing by the teacher, even very young students can begin to become adept at this thinking skill. |

The big idea seems to be...

METACOGNITIVE DISCUSSION

Ask students to complete the lead-in: Finding the "big idea" is like _____

Model the analogy: "Finding the big idea is like a belt because it brings things together."

CLOSURE

For homework, have students watch a particular TV show. Tell them to come in the next day ready to share the big ideas with a friend.

Meeting Metaphor

BACKGROUND	Based on the Gordon's Synectics Model, young children can be lead into comparisons to prepare them for metaphorical thinking. Giving them ample opportunity to find similarities in very different-looking objects forces them to make creative connections.
THINKING SKILL	Making Analogies
FOCUS ACTIVITY	Have students cut out pictures of eight things and paste them on a circle separated into eight equal sections. Put clock hands on the circles and have students take turns moving the hands to two different pictures.

Then ask them to find ways that the two pictures are similar. For example, both are useful, are clear, have something in them, etc. Lots of practice in forcing relationships will help students see comparisons that are necessary for using metaphors.

OBJECTIVE

To use comparisons to develop metaphorical thinking.

INPUT

1. Direct Analogy: Simple comparison.
   In direct analogy, the student compares one thing to another thing through the use of metaphor or simile.

   a. Metaphor - Example: the seed of the idea

   b. Simile - Example: An idea is like a seed.

2. Explain that now the students will be using different comparisons. They will not have pictures, but must use their minds and create pictures as they try to make connections with some unusual comparisons.

ACTIVITY

Use some of the following synectics examples or make up your own. Also probe students' thinking to find out why they answered in a particular way. In telling why, we can hear the comparisons they are making and reasonings they are using.

Set 1:

A broom is like what animal? Why?
An elephant is like what machine? Why?
A promise is like what electrical appliance? Why?
A computer is like what natural occurence in nature? Why?

Set 2:

Would you rather be:
a giant redwood or a tiny ladybug? Why?
a river or an ocean? Why?
a french fry or a cookie? Why?
a snowflake or a secret cave? Why?
a star or a dream? Why?

Set 3:

Which is funnier - jello or mashed potatoes? Why?
Which is quicker - black or white? Why?
Which is louder - a hiccup or an alarm clock? Why?
Which is thinner - summer or winter? Why?
Which lasts longer - a friend or an enemy? Why?

Set 4:

A clock is like a window because both...
A bike is like music because both...
Laughter is like a safe because both...
A thought is like a rainbow because...
A wish is like _____ because...

METACOGNITIVE DISCUSSION

Have students tell a partner about the hardest comparison—the one they had some trouble making.

CLOSURE

Do a quick wrap-around with this lead-in: The big idea is...

Start Them Problem Solving and Decision Making

Canned Collectibles

BACKGROUND

Recipe for Reasoning:
Canned Collectibles

I hear and I forget.
I see and I remember.
I do and I understand.

(Chinese Proverb)

To help young children internalize the concepts of higher order thinking, concrete objects can be wonderful learning tools. By actually doing the sequencing, classifying and comparing with hands-on manipulatives, the concepts will crystallize for them.

THINKING SKILL

Problem Solving

FOCUS ACTIVITY

Ask students to bring cans of all sizes and things to put in them. Send a note home to parents suggesting appropriate contributions. Explain that these items will become the "canned collectibles" for use during math time and for reasoning and thinking activities throughout the school year. As you collect the assortments of cans and collectibles, begin to assemble them for the various activities. (See Input.)

OBJECTIVE

To use concrete manipulatives to introduce higher-order thinking skills.

INPUT

Utensils: Cans with lids of every size and shape; coffee cans, lemonade cans, peanut cans, cat food cans, anything you can.

Ingredients: Small objects found around the house, garage, office, attic, or cellar.

> *KNEAD*...the nuts and bolts, nails, and noodles
> *BLEND*...the beans, buttons, and beads
> *MIX*...the magnets, matchbox cars, and marbles
> *CUT IN*...ceramic tiles, canning jar rubbers, and caps
> *FRY*...feathers, forks, and finger rings
> *SPRINKLE* ...pipe cleaners, pennies, and Popsicle sticks
> *COVER*...the clothes pins, clips, and cones
> *STIR*...all objects of one type together
> *SET*...into containers covered with colored contact paper
> *SEAL*...with plastic lids
> *STORE*...in conspicuous spots, easily accessible to students

---

ACTIVITY

Serving Suggestions: "Canned Collectibles" enhance the flavor of:

Memory:

1. COUNT by 2's, 3's, 5's, 10's, etc.

2. RECALL all the objects that were placed on a tray (after they have been removed).

3. LOCATE the one item that has been removed after viewing the assortment for several seconds.

Cognition Exercises:

1. SEQUENCE items from largest to smallest; dullest to brightest; hardest to softest; loudest to quietest...

2. COMPUTE by making addition and subtraction problems...

3. SORT into three groups and tell how you decided.

Convergent Thinking:

1. CLASSIFY by sizes, shapes, colors, textures...

2. FIND the heaviest can; most mysterious can...tell why.

3. DEMONSTRATE story problems with the canned items.

Divergent Production:

1. CREATE a design with your canned collectibles.

2. COMBINE your collectibles with a partner's and INVENT a game.

3. ESTIMATE how many items are in your can; check your answer.

Evaluation Tasks:

1. COMPARE your canned collectibles with a partner's; note the similarities and differences. Use a Venn diagram to help you "reason" out your answers.

2. Use the INQUIRY METHOD to determine what's in your partner's can.

3. DETERMINE five qualities of your object groupings. (Three or four students can work together to assemble some different groupings of the objects. Mix up the cans.)

METACOGNITIVE DISCUSSION

After each activity, ask students to discuss "Mrs. Potter's Questions":

1. What was I supposed to do?

2. What did I do well?

3. What would I do differently next time?

4. What help do I need?

CLOSURE

Use a wrap-around for each activity:

1. I think...

2. The hardest part was...

3. The thing I liked most was...

Shoe Box Curriculum

BACKGROUND

The shoe box curriculum capsulizes a language arts program which is based on a child's innermost feelings: feelings evidenced in words that are vibrant and alive and personal; words pulled from life, from way down deep in their insides; words that evoke immediate and vivid mental images for that child; words that become a part of that child from the moment of experience; words that reawaken a part of that child with each repeated reading. These words have a genuine and appropriate relevancy for that child. And it is this relevancy that insures success-oriented experiences with the reasoning processes that follow.

THINKING SKILL

Higher-Order Thinking

FOCUS ACTIVITY

Ask the children to bring in shoe boxes of different sizes and shapes. When each child has a box, spend some time decorating the boxes with pictures of their favorite things—favorite food, insect, flower, etc. These images will be the catalysts for developing their personal key vocabulary.

OBJECTIVE

To develop higher-order thinking skills.

INPUT

Words are like shoes! One size doesn't fit all. We have preferences in styles and colors to fit our functions and fancies. We are individuals!

Materials

Shoe boxes from home, multi-colored word card strips, markers.

Procedure

Through an experiential language approach, students accumulate a shoe box of personalized vocabulary cards which become the tattered treasures of their learning. Try this daily routine:

1. As children arrive, they get their boxes and play "Fish" with a partner.

2. As they finish, they meet with the teacher, who quickly flashes the child's words. (Color-coded monthly to keep the number of words manageable.) Only "one-look" words are kept; others are discarded.

3. The child says his special word request for that day.

4. The teacher writes it on the colored strip, while repeating the word.

5. The child traces the word with his or her finger and vocalizes its name.

6. The child then "studies" his new word with paint, clay, chalk, etc.

7. After studying the word, the child uses it in an original story. These will be short in the beginning, but progress in this kind of experiential writing is fast.

8. The word is then placed in the shoe box. Current words are kept in the front of the box. All others are filed alphabetically for future reference. This is a working file for each child.

ACTIVITY

Comment: The "Shoe Box Curriculum" is a program to inspire children to begin their journey into the mysterious world of reading, writing, and reasoning. It is a teaching tool that unlocks magnificent unknown resources within their young minds. It provides a delicate glimpse into the wonderfully real and imaginary worlds of children as it chronicles their passage from the spoken word to the written form and into the world of reading and reasoning. And, above all, it is the art of language and the science of reasoning in its splendid uniqueness as only these young ones could express it.

IMITATE! INNOVATE! INVENT!
THIS IDEA IS VERSATILE!

Reasoning With A Shoe Box (A beginning)

Memory:
SAY "one-look" words to a friend.
SKETCH a configuration of today's word.
LIST all the "moving" words (verbs).
SEQUENCE some sentences (structure and restructure sentences with the moveable cards).

Cognition:
CLASSIFY: things, qualities...
ALPHABETIZE your words in your shoe box
SORT for rhyming words; antonyms; synonyms...
FIND a friend who has three of the same words you have.

Convergent Production:
EXPLAIN why you chose a certain word...
DESCRIBE your "fattest" word; tell why you think so.
SEARCH for your longest word; shortest; funniest...
PRODUCE three sentences using five nouns from your box.

Divergent Production:
CREATE a picture to illustrate a part of your story.
REARRANGE your words into three special groups. Tell why.
COMBINE two words to make a new, original word. Tell the meaning.
IMAGINE what this newly created word looks, smells, feels, and sounds like. Use all of your senses to help describe it.

Evaluation:
COMPARE how two words are alike and different.
DECIDE which words have the most "hang-down" letters.
SELECT your best word. Tell why.
ANALYZE two words and tell how they are related. Then find a similar set to match. Now you have an analogy.

METACOGNITIVE DISCUSSION

Throughout the program described on the previous page, following a particular activity on analyzing or evaluating, ask students to reflect on their thinking. For example: What did you learn? Was this easy or difficult to do?

CLOSURE

The closure for each activity can focus on the kind of thinking that is required.

Examples:
Comparing words is like _____ .
Trying to decide on the "fattest" word was _____.

Use your imagination to develop a lead-in appropriate to the task.

Twenty Pairs = Twenty Lines

BACKGROUND

When presented with a challenge or problem, the degree of success can depend on many factors. However, there are four skills that are useful for problem solving, the ability to:

> observe
> organize
> take a risk
> accept the possibility of multiple solutions

These skills can be learned and practiced, thus improving problem-solving approaches.

THINKING SKILL

Problem Solving

FOCUS ACTIVITY

Ask students to talk in a wrap-around about some things that come in pairs.

OBJECTIVE

To solve a problem by observing spatial positions and spatial limitations.

INPUT

Give each child a paper which has 20 or fewer pairs of letters, numerals, or symbols. If children are older or more capable, use words from social studies, vocabulary lists, spelling lists, seasons, nouns, or pronouns — whatever relates to your content curriculum.

ACTIVITY

Find the pairs, then draw lines connecting the pairs.

Discuss: What do you see in the large square?
The task is to draw a line matching each of the 20 pairs. (Do one example.)

There are three rules:

1. You *cannot* go outside of the square.

2. You *cannot* cross over any line

3. You *cannot* go through a letter.

You may use colored pencils or crayons. Ask: Why would this be helpful?

Suggestion: prepare extra copies for children who do not succeed and will want to try again.

Allow children to work on the task. Observe individual approaches.

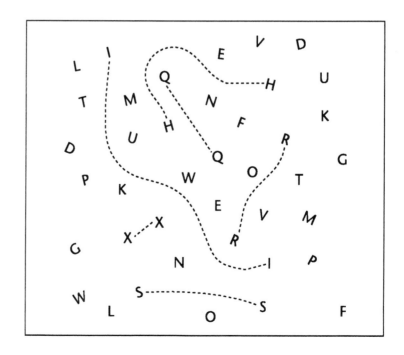

METACOGNITIVE DISCUSSION

Ask children who completed the task to share:

1. Where did you begin? Why?

2. What did you look for?

3. What made this task hard?

4. What made this task easy?

Ask children who did *not* complete the task:

1. Show me where you got in trouble...What was in the way?

2. How could you get around the trouble?

3. Next time, which lines would you draw first? Why?

4. Which match looks like it is the easiest?

5. Which match looks like it is the most difficult?

How many different ways do you think we could make matches?

CLOSURE

Using a new piece of paper, have children draw a large rectangle and put 10 pairs of numbers somewhere inside of the shape. Have them trade with a neighbor and make matches observing the same rules.

It's a Problem!

BACKGROUND

We can observe young children problem solving as infants. If a brightly colored distant object attracts a child, body movement begins as the child squirms, crawls, or walks to reach the object. If an infant confronts a "brick wall" in his path, he will investigate how to get through, over, around, or under it. A "brick wall" need not be a physical barrier; daily problems can be "brick walls." Take time to reflect on the creative problem solving young children do in play and in uncountable flashes of curiosity.

When children become students, we must capitalize on their natural problem-solving skill by verbalizing, identifying, sharing solutions, and promoting reasoned judgments. We cannot expect logical decision making from young adults if we don't begin early to teach them how to recognize a problem and what to do with it. Alex F. Osborn in *Applied Imagination* offers an effective model for problem solving.

We can begin this model with young children. As in learning sentence structure, students need to master simple sentences before compound and complex sentences can be understood.

THINKING SKILL

Problem Solving

FOCUS ACTIVITY

Set up a barrier in the classroom and have the students figure out ways to get around it.

OBJECTIVE   To identify a problem and discover multiple solutions.

INPUT   Share this short story with the students.

You have accepted your first "dog-sitting" job for your neighbors who took a weekend trip to their cottage. Their dog will be staying in their garage. You agreed to feed and walk the dog early each morning and again each evening. They left while you were at school, and now it is 6 o'clock Friday evening. As you leave your house to take care of the dog, you realize the key for your neighbor's garage is in your desk at school.

ACTIVITY   Ask: What is your biggest problem?

Children need to identify the primary problem of "how to take care of the dog." The key being in school *is* a problem, but not the primary one!! Ask clarifying questions leading children to the real problem.

Once established, record the primary problem on chart paper. Brainstorm solutions (follow guidelines: defer judgment, offbeat ideas are welcome, vast number, expand on ideas by piggybacking).

It is not necessary to arrive at just one solution to a problem such as this.

Teachers are faced with dozens of problems every day. Once we tackle the skills of problem solving, there are classroom situations that can be solved by children with the process of identifying the problem, brainstorming multiple solutions, and (when appropriate) agreeing on the best solution(s).

Children who are allowed and encouraged to discuss situational problems in the classroom will transfer the process more easily and be better prepared to participate in decision making at a later age. If children rarely discuss or solve problems in their primary years, how prepared will they be when problem solving is a prerequisite for achieving and succeeding?

Practical and proven uses: Early problem-solving, carefully presented and practiced, will minimize some of the daily classroom disruptions:

"I don't have a pencil."
"I forgot my library book."
"I haven't got any paper."
"My mom forgot to give me my gym shoes."

METACOGNITIVE DISCUSSION

Do a language experience chart.

A PROBLEM IS:

When it rains on July 4th.
When I lose my lunch money.

CLOSURE

Introduce a group PNI activity, which encourages decisions with considerable latitude. The list of solutions to any situational problem provides an excellent opportunity to practice PNI. If children are young or not familiar with PNI, you need to explain the use of Positive as "yes, that might work," Negative as "no, I don't think it will work," and Interesting as "maybe."

Take one item at a time and get a consensus of how the solution should be rated. If children are old enough, allow them the opportunity to do this in a small cooperative group, with a partner, or in their own LOGS. How you use PNI depends on your class. Modeling it early will encourage use in multiple situations.

The Human Graph

BACKGROUND

Decisions! Decisions! Decisions! What to wear? Who to play with? When? What to do? Thousands of decisions are made each day by each of us, including young children. How do we go about the decision-making process? How do we become sound decision-makers? What can we do to help young students become aware of their decision-making processes? In what ways can we help students analyze their manner of making choices so they can call upon successful strategies when needed? The Human Graph provides a visible, breathing, moving, and challenging record of the decision-making process. Students begin to consciously explore the intricacies of their thinking as they exercise their capacities for weighing alternatives, evaluating other points of view, and advocating their opinions and ideas. The Human Graph is the sort of strategy that can be used any time a choice or decision situation arises.

THINKING SKILL

Making Decisions

FOCUS ACTIVITY

Ask students to choose which they would prefer:

1. A pet dog or cat.

2. Chocolate or vanilla ice cream.

3. A boat ride or a plane ride.

Elicit synonyms for the word "decisions." Elicit examples of times when students must make choices and decisions.

Explain that you have a game that will give them practice in deciding what they will be playing today and during the entire school year.

OBJECTIVE

To foster thoughtful decision making.

INPUT

Draw an imaginary line dividing the room into segments (or actually place masking tape on the floor with the appropriate markings). Assign headings to the line.

AGREE
NOT SURE
DISAGREE

(DISAGREE) or CHOICE #1	(NOT SURE) or CHOICE #2	(AGREE) or CHOICE #3

ACTIVITY

To use the Human Graph as a teaching strategy, simply stand in the center of the room and have students cluster in front of you. Pose the question as you indicate the side for each choice: Would you rather_____ or _____? (Start with just two choices - Agree or Disagree.) Be sure to ask students *why* they agree or disagree.

Would you rather be: a smile or a frown?
                       a sail boat or a piece of chalk?
                       a pencil or a pair of shoes?
                       a jogger or a heartbeat?
                       a turtle or a rabbit?

Watch as they move to one side or the other. Then ask why they made their choice. Listen! Permit time for each student to explain his or her decision. WAIT! Let the child fully develop the depth of his or her thoughts as he or she discovers the connection between decision and experiences. Allow movement caused by students changing their minds, but also encourage them to advocate their opinions and convictions. Continue to move through the graph in a similar manner sampling as many ideas as time permits. Be sure to balance opposing opinions.

METACOGNITIVE DISCUSSION

Decisions are made moment by moment. Experience and examine the processes with the children. First, get them to think. Then, get them to think about their thinking as they explore the metacognitive realms. Give them opportunities to ponder their patterns for thinking. Take advantage of those teachable moments!

As the human graph evolves, be aware of and ultimately discuss with the students: how quickly one reaches a decision; how far to one side one moves; how often one changes one's mind; how one comes to one's decision; how one reacts in a minority/majority position; and how one reflects one's attitudes in one's choices.

CLOSURE

Make a Log entry. Choose one of the lead-ins:

1. Making decisions is like _____ because _____.

2. The Human Graph today looked like this:

3. My problem with choosing is _____.

TIPS FOR TEACHING THINKING

by Robin Fogarty & Jim Bellanca

TEACH thinking by modeling; demonstrate and label critical and creative thinking as it occurs.

EXPECT all students to think skillfully; be aware of implied messages; believe that *all kids can.*

ASK questions that cause "something to go on inside the student's head."

CREATE cooperative groups and thinking/pair/share partners for processing information; invite student-to-student interaction.

HELP students process strategies metacognitively; help them think about their learning and thinking by planning, monitoring, and evaluating with them.

TOLERATE noise, movement, and "failures"; a thinking classroom is a busy place.

HAVE fun! Your enthusiasm for learning is contagious in the classroom; the kids will catch it.

INVITE multiple responses to carefully designed, divergent questions; ask how and why questions.

NURTURE thinking by arranging your classroom to encourage intense, involved student interactions.

KEEP silent! Use wait-time — a 3-10 second pause after asking a question; let them think.

INSIST on intelligent behaviors by guiding students to make their own decisions and solve their own problems.

NEVER stop moving; teacher mobility in the classroom impacts positively on student interaction.

GIVE the kids responsibility for their own learning; don't tell them; involve them.

BIBLIOGRAPHY

Ainsworth-Land, V., & Fletcher, N. (1979). *Making waves with creative problem solving.* New York: D.O.K.

Anderson, R. C., et al. (1985). *Becoming a nation of readers. The report of the Commission on Reading.* Pittsburgh, PA: National Academy of Education.

Archibald-Marcus, S., & Bellanca, J. (1988). *Early stars: Skills for saying "yes" to health (K-5).* Palatine, IL: Skylight Publishing.

Archibald-Marcus, S., & McDonald, P. (1990). *Tools for the cooperative classroom.* Palatine, IL: Skylight Publishing.

Bellanca, J. (1991). *Building a caring, cooperative classroom.* Palatine, IL: Skylight Publishing.

Bellanca, J. (1990). *The cooperative think tank: Graphic organizers to teach thinking in the cooperative classroom.* Palatine, IL: Skylight Publishing.

Bellanca, J. (1990). *Keep them thinking (Level III).* Palatine, IL: Skylight Publishing.

Bellanca, J. (1989). *Team stars: Skills for deciding together (6-8).* Palatine, IL: Skylight Publishing.

Bellanca, J., Castagna, C., & Archibald-Marcus, S. (1990). *Star parents: Skills for effective parenting.* Palatine, IL: Skylight Publishing.

Bellanca, J., & Fogarty, R. (1991). *Blueprints for thinking in the cooperative classroom.* (2nd Ed.). Palatine, IL: Skylight Publishing.

Bellanca, J., & Fogarty, R. (1986). *Catch them thinking: A handbook of classroom strategies.* Palatine, IL: Skylight Publishing.

Bellanca, J., & Johnson, T. (1989). *Star choices: Skills for saying no (9-12).* Palatine, IL: Skylight Publishing.

Beyer, B. (1985, January). Teaching thinking skills: How the principal can know they are being taught. *NASSP Bulletin.*

Beyer, B. (1984, November). Common sense about teaching thinking skills. *Educational Leadership,* pp. 57-62.

Beyer, B. (1984, March). Improving thinking skills—defining the problem. *Phi Delta Kappan*, p. 486-490.

Biondi, A. (Ed.). (1972). *The creative process.* New York: D.O.K.

Bloom, B. (1981). *All our children learning: A primer for parents, teachers, and educators.* London: McGraw-Hill.

Bloom, B. S. (Ed.). (1956). *Taxonomy of educational objectives: Cognitive domain.* New York: David McKay.

Burns, M. (1976). *The book of think or how to solve a problem twice your size.* Boston: Little, Brown & Co.

Burns, M. (1975). *I hate mathematics.* Boston: Little, Brown & Co.

Campbell, T. C., et al. (1980). A teacher's guide to the learning cycle: A Piagetian-based approach to college instruction. In R. G. Fuller, et al. (Eds.), *Piagetian programs in higher education.* (p. 27-46). Lincoln, NE: ADAPT, University of Nebraska-Lincoln.

Carpenter, E. T. (1980). Piagetian interviews of college students. In R. G. Fuller, et al. (Eds.), *Piagetian programs in higher education.* (p. 15-21). Lincoln, NE: ADAPT, University of Nebraska-Lincoln.

Carpenter, T. P., Corbitt, M. K., Kepner, H., Lindquist, M. M., & Reys, R. W. (1980). Problem solving in mathematics: National assessment results. *Educational Leadership, 37,* 562-563.

Chase, L. (1975). *The other side of the report card.* Glenview, IL: Scott Foresman.

Clark, B. (1992). *Growing up gifted: Developing the potential of children at home and at school.* New York: MacMillan.

Clement, J. (1982). Algebra word problem solutions: Thought processes underlying a common misconception. *Journal for Research in Mathematics Education, 13,* 16-30.

Clement, J. (1982). Students' preconceptions in introductory mechanics. *American Journal of Physics, 50,* 66-71.

College Entrance Examination Board. (1983). *Academic preparation for college: What students need to know and be able to do.* New York: College Board.

Costa, A. (1991). *The school as a home for the mind.* Palatine, IL: Skylight Publishing.

Costa, A. (Ed.). (1985). *Developing minds.* Alexandria, VA: ASCD.

Costa, A., Bellanca, J., & Fogarty R. (Eds.) (1992). *If minds matter: A foreword to the future (Vols. I & II).* Palatine, IL: Skylight Publishing.

de Bono, E. (1973). *Lateral thinking: Creativity step by step.* New York: Harper and Row.

Easterling, J., & Pasanen, J. (1979). *Confront, construct, complete.* Rochelle Park, NJ: Hayden.

Eberle, B., & Stanish, B. (1980). *CPS for kids.* Buffalo, NY: D.O.K.

Eberle, R. F. (1971). *SCAMPER games for imagination development.* Buffalo, NY: D.O.K.

Eberle, B. (1982). *Visual thinking.* Buffalo, NY: D.O.K.

Edwards, B. (1979). *Drawing on the right side of the brain.* Los Angeles: J.P. Tarcher.

ESS Science Series. *Problem cards: Attribute games and problems.* New York: McGraw-Hill.

Eggen, P., & Kauchak, D. (1979). *Strategies for teachers: Teaching content and thinking skills.* Englewood Cliffs, NJ: Prentice-Hall.

Eisner, E. W. (1983, October). The kinds of schools we need. *Educational Leadership.*

Elbow, P. (1981). *Writing with power: Techniques for mastering the writing process.* New York: Oxford University Press.

Elbow, P. (1973). *Writing without teachers.* New York: Oxford University Press.

Ferguson, M. (1980). *The Aquarian conspiracy: Personal and social transformation in the 1980s.* Los Angeles: J.P. Tarcher.

Feuerstein, R. (1980). *Instrumental enrichment.* Baltimore: University Park Press.

Fogarty, R. (1991). *How to integrate the curricula.* Palatine, IL: Skylight Publishing.

Fogarty, R. (1990). *Designs for cooperative interaction.* Palatine, IL: Skylight Publishing.

Fogarty, R. (1990). *Keep them thinking (Level II).* Palatine, IL: Skylight Publishing.

Fogarty, R., & Bellanca, J. (1987). *Patterns for thinking: Patterns for transfer.* Palatine, IL: Skylight Publishing.

Fogarty, R., & Bellanca, J. (1986). *Teach them thinking.* Palatine, IL: Skylight Publishing.

Fogarty, R., & Haack, J. (1988). *The thinking/writing connection: A thinker's log (6-12).* Palatine, IL: Skylight Publishing.

Fogarty, R., & Haack, J. (1986). *The thinking log (K-6).* Palatine, IL: Skylight Publishing.

Fogarty, R., Perkins, D., & Barell, J. (1992). *How to teach for transfer.* Palatine, IL: Skylight Publishing.

Gallagher, J. J. (1985). *Teaching the gifted child.* Boston: Allyn & Bacon.

Gallelli, G. (1977). *Activity mindset guide.* New York: D.O.K.

Gardner, H. (1983). *Frames of mind: The theory of multiple intelligences.* New York: Basic Books.

Glatthorn, A. (1984). *Differentiated supervision.* Alexandria, VA: ASCD.

Good, T. (1981, February). Teacher expectations and student perceptions. *Educational Leadership.*

Goodlad, J. I. (1984). *A place called school: Prospects for the future.* New York: McGraw Hill.

Guilford, J. P. (1975). *Way beyond I.Q.* Buffalo, NY: Creative Education Foundation.

Johnson, R., & Johnson, D. (1991). *Learning together and alone: Cooperative, competitive, and individualistic learning.* Englewood Cliffs, NJ: Prentice Hall.

Johnson, R., & Johnson, D. (1984). *Circles of learning.* Alexandria, VA: ASCD.

Johnson, R., & Johnson, D. (1982, October). Cooperation in learning: Ignored but powerful. *Lyceum.*

Karplus, R. (1974). *Science curriculum improvement study: Teacher's handbook.* Berkeley, CA: University of California.

Larkin, J. H., McDermott, J., Simon, D. P., & Simon, H. A. (1980). Expert and novice performance in solving physics problems. *Science, 208,* 1335-1342.

Lazear, D. (1991). *Seven ways of knowing.* Palatine, IL: Skylight Publishing.

Lazear, D. (1991). *Seven ways of teaching.* Palatine, IL: Skylight Publishing.

Machado, L. A. (1980). *The right to be intelligent.* New York: Pergamon Press.

Maraviglia, C. (1978). *Creative problem-solving think book.* Buffalo, NY: D.O.K.

McCloskey, M., Carmazza, A., & Green, B. (1980). Curvilinear motion in the absence of external forces: Naive beliefs about the motion of objects. *Science, 210,* 1130-1141.

National Commission on Excellence in Education. (1983). *A nation at risk: The imperative for educational reform.* Washington, D.C.: Department of Education.

Nickerson, R. S. (1982). *Understanding understanding.* (BBN Report No. 5087).

Nickerson, R. S. (1983). Computer programming as a vehicle for teaching thinking skills. *Journal of Philosophy for children, 4,* 3-4.

Nickerson, R. S., Perkins, D. N., & Smith, E. E. (1984). *Teaching thinking.* (BBN Report No. 5575).

Nickerson, R. S., Salter, W., Shepard, & Herrnstein, J. (1984). *The teaching of learning strategies.* (BBN Report 5578).

Nisbett, R., & Ross, L. (1980). *Human inference: Strategies and shortcomings of social judgment.* Englewood Cliffs, NJ: Prentice-Hall.

Noller, R., Parnes, S., & Biondi, A. (1976). *Creative action book.* New York: Scribner.

Noller, R., Treffinger, D., & Houseman, E. (1979). *It's a gas to be gifted or CPS for the gifted and talented.* Buffalo, NY: D.O.K.

Noller, R. (1977). *Scratching the surface of creative problem solving: A bird's eye view of CPS.* Buffalo, NY: D.O.K.

Opeka, K. (1989). *Keep them thinking.* (Level I). Palatine, IL: Skylight Publishing.

Osborn, A. F. (1953). *Applied imagination: Principles and procedures of creative thinking.* New York: Scribner.

Parnes, S. (1975). *Aha! Insights into creative behavior.* Buffalo, NY: D.O.K.

Parnes, S. (1972). *Creativity: Unlocking human potential.* Buffalo, NY: D.O.K.

Pearson, C. (1980, February). Can you keep quiet for three minutes? *Learning.*

Peters, T., & Austin, N. (1985). *Passion for excellence.* New York: Random House.

Peters, T., & Waterman, R., Jr. (1982). *In search of excellence.* New York: Harper & Row.

Polette, N. (1981). *Picture books for gifted programs.* Metuchen, NJ: Scarecrow Press.

Raths, L., et al. (1986). *Teaching for thinking: Theory, strategies, and activities for the classroom.* New York: Teachers College Press.

Rico, G. L. (1983). *Writing the natural way.* Boston: J.P. Tarcher.

Rowe, M. B. (1989). Science, silence and sanctions. *Science & Children, 6,* 11-13.

Scardamalia, M., Bereiter, C., & Fillion, B. (1979). *The little red writing book: A source book of consequential writing activities.* Ontario, Canada: Pedagogy of Writing Project, O.I.S.E.

Schoenfeld, A. H. (1980). Teaching problem-solving skills. *American Mathematical Monthly, 87*(10): 794-805.

Smith, F. (1986). *Insult to intelligence: The bureaucratic invasion of our classroom.* New York: Arbor House.

Sternberg, R. J. (1984, September). How can we teach intelligence? *Educational Leadership.*

Sternberg, R. J. (1981, October). Intelligence as thinking and learning skills. *Educational Leadership,* 18-20.

Torrance, E. P. (1979). *The search for satori and creativity.* Buffalo, NY: Creative Education Foundation and Great Neck, NY: Creative Synergetics Associates.

Trowbridge, D. E., & McDermott, L. C. (1980). Investigation of student understanding of the concept of velocity in one dimension. *American Journal of Physics, 48*(12), 1010-1028.

Tversky, A., & Kahneman, D. (1974). Judgment under uncertainty: Heuristics and biases. *Science, 185,* 1124-1131.

Underwood, V. L. (1982). *Self-management skills for college students: A program in how to learn.* Unpublished doctoral dissertation, University of Texas.

U.S. Department of Education. (1986). *What works: Research about teaching and learning.* Washington, D.C.: Author.

von Oech, R. (1986). *A kick in the seat of the pants.* New York: Harper and Row.

von Oech, R. (1983). *A whack on the side of the head.* New York: Warner Books.

Wallace, R., & Editors of Time-Life Books. (1966). *The world of Leonardo. 1452 - 1519.* New York: Time Incorporated (Time Life Library of Art).

Warner, S. A. (1972). *Teacher.* New York: Vintage Books.

Wason, P. C. (1974). The psychology of deceptive problems. *New Scientist, 63,* 382-385.

Wayman, J. (1981). *The other side of reading.* Carthage, IL: Good Apple.

Weber, P. (1978). *Promote...Discovering ways to learn and research.* Buffalo, NY: D.O.K.

Weber, P. (1978). *Question quest: Discovering ways to ask worthwhile questions.* Buffalo, NY: D.O.K.

Weinstein, C. E., & Underwood, V. L. (1983). Learning strategies: The how of learning. In J. Segal, S. Chipman, & R. Glaser (Eds.), *Relating instruction to basic research.* Hillsdale, NJ: Lawrence Erlbaum.

Whimbey, A. (1975). *Intelligence can be taught.* New York: Innovative Science.

Williams, F. E. (1970). *Classroom ideas for encouraging thinking and feeling.* Buffalo, NY: D.O.K.

There are

one-story intellects,

two-story intellects, and three-story

intellects with skylights. All fact collectors, who

have no aim beyond their facts, are one-story men. Two-story men

compare, reason, generalize, using the labors of the fact collectors as

well as their own. Three-story men idealize, imagine,

predict—their best illumination comes from

above, through the skylight.

—*Oliver Wendell*

Holmes

SkyLight
Training and Publishing Inc.